Budgeting for the Broke Paycheck

A Realistic System When There's More Month Than Money

Marcus Trevelyan

First edition, 2026

Published by Marcus Trevelyan

Contents

Chapter 1: The Red Zone: When Paycheck Doesn't Cover Bills

Sarah works sixty hours a week between Target and freelance cleaning gigs she picks up through an app. She makes $2,400 a month when both income streams are humming. Her rent is $1,350. Utilities: $180. Groceries for three people: $450 if she's careful. Every single month, she is $753 short before she even starts.

The math doesn't work. It's not close.

The first of the month always *feels* good, though. That brief window after the direct deposits hit and her account balance shows four digits instead of two. Sarah told me she'll actually check her banking app multiple times that day, just to see the number. It's like a high. A fleeting one. Because within two weeks, the anxiety starts creeping back in. Groceries get trimmed—name brands swapped for store brands, fresh fruit replaced with canned. Entertainment gets cut entirely; movie night becomes whatever's already on Netflix. By the third week, she's in triage mode. Which bill can slide until the next paycheck? Can the electric company wait five more days? What about the car insurance—how long after the due date before they actually cancel the policy?

It's not a lack of effort. Sarah isn't careless. She tracks *some* expenses, usually whatever she can remember to jot down after a twelve-hour day when her brain feels like static. But it's chaotic, reactive, always playing defense. She'll get a low balance alert on her phone—that gut-punch notification at 9:47 PM—and scramble to transfer $40 from her savings account (which has $127 in it) to checking. It buys her a day, maybe two. Then the cycle repeats. Late fees. Overdraft charges. A $35 penalty because a payment processed one day early and she didn't have the buffer.

Sarah isn't unique. Not even close.

I've talked to hundreds of people in versions of this situation. Different cities, different jobs, different family structures—but the same core problem. They're working more than one job, stretching every dollar, making sacrifices that would break most people, and still finding themselves in what I call "the red zone." That's the period between paychecks where expenses outweigh income. Where you're functionally underwater, just treading water until the next deposit hits. It feels awful. Suffocating. And it's shockingly common.

You might think the answer is simple: earn more. Just get a better job, pick up another side gig, hustle harder. And sure, more income helps—we'll talk about that in Chapter 8. But here's what most people miss: the issue often isn't *how much* you make. It's *how* you manage what you have when income is unevenly distributed and expenses are relentless. Sarah isn't spending recklessly. She's prioritizing her kids. She's keeping the lights on. She's doing everything "right" according to conventional wisdom. She just lacks a system to proactively account for those dips between paychecks. The gaps. The holes where the math stops adding up.

And those gaps are getting wider.

The nature of modern finances magnifies the problem. Everything feels instant now. Bills are due immediately—sometimes they pull the payment a day *early* and wreck your carefully constructed math. Subscriptions auto-renew without asking permission. Small purchases vanish into the ether because you're tapping a card, not counting out cash. It's friction-free spending, which sounds great until you realize friction was the only thing slowing you down. Sarah told me she often feels like her money "disappears" before she can actually *see* it working for her. It's in her account for a moment, then it's gone, swallowed by automatic withdrawals and immediate obligations. That sense of powerlessness—of watching your paycheck evaporate in real time—is what drives the stress. The sleepless nights. The constant low-grade anxiety that follows you everywhere.

Most budgeting advice completely misses this reality.

I'm serious. Go pick up any mainstream personal finance book. I'll wait. Notice how they all assume you have margin to work with? They're written for people who are already covering their bills and just need to *optimize*. They'll tell you to allocate 50% to needs, 30% to wants, 20% to savings. Great. What do you do when your needs are already 110% of your income? They'll suggest building an emergency fund of three to six months' expenses. Fantastic. What about the emergency happening *right now*, the one due in five days that you can't cover?

That's not an optimization problem. It's a triage problem. And it needs different tools.

I know what you're thinking. You've heard this before. Another book promising to fix your financial problems with some revolutionary new system. Another expert who doesn't understand what it's like to be $340 short on the 18th of the month, staring at a disconnect notice from the power company.

Here's the thing: I do understand. Not theoretically—actually.

I grew up watching my mom navigate this exact situation. Single parent, two kids, working as a home health aide pulling overnight shifts because they paid an extra $2.75 an hour. I remember being nine years old and answering the phone when the creditors called. I got good at saying, "She's not home right now, can I take a message?" even when she was standing right there in the kitchen, shaking her head. I remember the notice taped to our door when the landlord started eviction proceedings because we were eight days late on rent. Not eight weeks. Eight *days*. I remember my mom sitting at the kitchen table at midnight with a calculator, a stack of bills, and a paycheck that was already spent before it hit her account.

She wasn't irresponsible. She worked her ass off. She just didn't have a system for the red zone—for the triage decisions that come when the math doesn't work. Nobody taught her how to prioritize when everything feels urgent. How to negotiate for breathing room. How to find money in places she didn't know to look.

That's what this book is about. Not deprivation. Not telling you to skip lattes or cancel Netflix or bootstrap your way to wealth. It's about building systems that work when you're already underwater. When you don't have margin. When the standard advice doesn't apply because your reality is fundamentally different.

Because here's what the personal finance gurus won't tell you: being broke is *expensive*. It costs money to be poor. Late fees. Overdraft charges. Higher insurance rates because you can't pay the full six-month premium upfront. Buying the cheap version of something that breaks in three months instead of the durable version that would last three years but costs more upfront. It's a tax on not having enough capital, and it compounds over time.

Sarah was paying $85 a month in fees. Just fees. Overdraft charges from timing mismatches. Late fees on bills that she *had* the money for, just not on the exact day they were due. A returned check fee when a cleaning client's payment bounced. That's $1,020 a year. Vanishing into the banking system. For nothing. For the crime of not having enough buffer.

That number made her physically ill when she calculated it. We sat in her kitchen—she'd offered me coffee, which I could tell she couldn't really afford to spare, but it felt important to her to offer—and she just stared at the total. "I could have bought my son the winter coat he needs," she said. "The good one that'll last him two years. Instead I bought the bank a whole lot of nothing."

The real cost of the red zone isn't just financial, though. That's what people miss when they talk about budgeting like it's a math problem. It's not. It's a stress problem. A mental health problem. A "lying awake at 3 AM running calculations in your head" problem.

Sarah described it as carrying a weight. A backpack full of rocks that she couldn't put down. It followed her to work, where she'd have to paste on a smile for customers while internally calculating whether she could push the car insurance payment to next week. It followed her home, where her daughter would ask if they could go to the movies and Sarah would have to say no, again, and watch her kid try to hide the disappointment. It followed her to bed, where she'd replay the day's expenses, wondering what she could have done differently, knowing she was already doing everything she could.

That weight grinds you down. It affects your health—stress hormones coursing through your system for weeks on end. It affects your relationships—you're short-tempered with the people you love because you're operating on fumes. It affects your work performance because part of your brain is always running budget calculations in the background. You're never fully present. Never fully *off*.

I watched this happen to my mom. She aged a decade in about three years. Started getting stress headaches that would knock her out for hours. Snapped at me and my sister over tiny things because she was already at her breaking point before we even opened our mouths.

It wasn't her fault. She was drowning. And nobody had thrown her a rope that actually reached.

The societal cost is bigger than we want to admit, too. When huge swaths of the population are stuck in survival mode—in the red zone—they can't invest in education. Can't start businesses. Can't take risks that might pay off long-term because they can't afford for anything to go wrong short-term. They can't move to where the better jobs are because moving costs money they don't have. Can't leave bad situations—bad jobs, bad relationships, bad living arrangements—because the alternative might be worse.

It perpetuates cycles. Kids growing up watching their parents stress about money absorb that anxiety, internalize the belief that financial security is something that happens to other people. I almost fell into that trap myself. It took a mentor in college pulling me aside and saying, "Your mom's situation doesn't have to be your situation" for me to even consider that escaping the red zone was possible.

So where do you actually start? Not with some app that gamifies your spending or a complicated spreadsheet with macros you don't understand. You start with visibility. Raw, unflinching visibility into where your money actually goes.

And I mean *actually*. Not where you think it goes. Not where it's supposed to go according to your mental math. Where it *goes*.

For the next thirty days, write down every single expense. I don't care if it's $0.75 for a pack of gum. Write it down. Get a notebook—a physical one, not an app. There's something about the physical act of writing that makes it stick. Sarah started doing this and said it felt almost ceremonial. Like she was creating a record. Bearing witness to her own financial reality.

Don't judge yourself during this phase. That's crucial. You're not tracking to shame yourself. You're tracking to gather data. Treat it like you're a scientist observing a subject. What are the patterns? Where are the leaks? What are you spending money on without even realizing it?

Sarah discovered she was spending $147 a month on convenience food. Frozen dinners. Fast food. Pre-made sandwiches from the gas station. Not because she was being lazy or irresponsible—because she was exhausted. She'd finish a ten-hour shift, pick up her kids, and the thought of cooking dinner felt impossible. So she'd grab something quick. Something easy. Something that added up to $147 a month.

That's not a moral failing. It's a logistics problem. When you're running on empty, of course you reach for convenience. The question isn't "Why am I doing this?"—the question is "What would need to change to make a different choice possible?"

For Sarah, it meant meal prepping on Sunday afternoons. Not elaborate recipes—just big batches of basics she could reheat. Rice and beans. Pasta with marinara. Chicken and vegetables. Stuff she could portion out and grab on her way out the door. It wasn't glamorous. But it freed up about $90 a month, which meant she could stop playing Russian roulette with the electric bill.

But here's where people usually push back. They say they don't have time to track expenses. Their spending is too erratic, too unpredictable. Life is too chaotic to write down every purchase.

I get it. I really do. Life *is* messy. Things come up. You're already stretched thin. But think about it this way: you probably spend more time scrolling social media—mindlessly, not even enjoying it—than it would take to track your expenses for ten minutes a day. I'm not saying that to shame you. I'm saying it because it's true. We all have time sinks that don't serve us. The question is whether you're willing to redirect fifteen minutes from one activity to another if it means finally getting out of the red zone.

Because the alternative—continuing in the pattern you're in now—has a cost. A real, quantifiable cost that you're paying every single day.

It's the $85 a month in fees. It's the interest accruing on debt you can't pay down because you're always in crisis mode. It's the opportunities you can't take—the job training program you can't afford, the slightly better apartment in a safer neighborhood, the reliable car that wouldn't break down and cost you a day's wages. It's the mental bandwidth you can't recover because you're always calculating, always worrying, always in triage.

Add that up over a year. Over five years. Over a lifetime.

Sarah did this calculation and it broke something open in her. She realized she'd spent the last six years—*six years*—paying the red zone tax. Fees, missed opportunities, health costs from stress-related issues. She estimated it had cost her somewhere north of $15,000. That's not nothing. That's a buffer. That's breathing room. That's a down payment on a different life.

And the worst part? It was preventable. Not easy to prevent—nothing about this is easy. But *possible*. With systems. With visibility. With tools designed for triage, not optimization.

So tonight, before you fall asleep, find a notebook. It doesn't have to be fancy. A $1.50 spiral from the drug store works fine. Open it to the first page. And write down three things you spent money on today. Just three. Don't judge them. Don't assign meaning. Just write them down.

Tomorrow, write down three more. Keep going. Build the habit. Because thirty days from now, you'll have data. Real data. Not guesses or assumptions or vague ideas about where your money goes. You'll know. And that knowledge—that visibility—is the foundation everything else is built on.

The categorization comes next. Understanding which expenses are truly essential and which ones are filling gaps created by exhaustion or lack of systems. Learning to tell the difference between "I need this" and "I need this *right now in this exact form*." Building a priority matrix so when you're $340 short, you know exactly which bill can wait and which one can't.

But we're getting ahead of ourselves. That's Chapter 3. Right now, the only thing you need to do is start tracking. Start building visibility. Start creating the foundation.

Because the red zone isn't a moral failure. It's not a character defect or a lack of willpower. It's a systems failure. You're running a complex operation—managing irregular income, fixed expenses, unexpected emergencies, and competing obligations—without the tools designed for that job. You've been handed the wrong equipment and told to make it work anyway.

This book is about getting you the right equipment. Starting with the ability to see clearly what's actually happening with your money, not what you think is happening or what you hope is happening. And then, piece by piece, building the systems that let you move from reactive scrambling to proactive planning. From the red zone to solid ground.

Sarah's not all the way there yet. She's four weeks into tracking, two weeks into meal prepping, one week into negotiating a payment plan with her car insurance company that spreads the cost out more evenly. She still has hard months. Still has weeks where the math is tight. But she told me something last week that stuck with me.

"I don't feel powerless anymore," she said. "The situation hasn't changed that much yet. But I don't feel like it's happening *to* me. I feel like I'm in the driver's seat, even if the car's not great and the road's bumpy. That shift—that's everything."

That shift starts with seeing clearly. With knowing your numbers. With tracking not to judge yourself but to understand the terrain you're actually navigating.

So grab that notebook. Write down those three expenses. And tomorrow, we'll start building the map of where your money actually flows—because you can't redirect a river until you know which direction it's running.

Sarah's gap—the space between what she earns and what she owes—is $753 every single month, and no amount of willpower or financial discipline can allocate money that isn't there.

The gap is real. The question isn't whether it exists—it's whether you can see through the fog of daily survival long enough to understand what's actually bleeding you dry.

Sarah lies awake at 2 AM doing mental math that never quite adds up—rent, utilities, groceries, the minimum payments she can't make—and the loop plays on repeat until her alarm goes off four hours later.

The math doesn't work. And no amount of cutting lattes or using coupons will change that structural fact. But there's something that does change it—and it starts with knowing exactly where the money you do have actually goes, not where you think it goes.

Chapter 2: Understanding Your Cash Flow: Beyond Income and Expenses

Where did your last paycheck actually go? Not where you think it went—where did it *actually* go? Can you name every charge?

I couldn't. For the better part of a year, I walked around convinced I was just fundamentally bad with money. Like some people are good at math and some aren't, some people can manage a budget and I... couldn't. That was the story I told myself. And it felt true, because no matter what I did, I was always short. Always scrambling. Always three days from overdraft and one unexpected expense from complete disaster.

My friend Sarah—we'd known each other since college, and she'd watched me stress about money for years without really knowing how to help—finally said something that changed everything. We were grabbing cheap tacos (because that's what you do when you're broke but still need to see another human being occasionally), and I was doing my usual spiral about how I'd overdrafted *again* and didn't understand *why* because I wasn't buying anything crazy, just normal stuff, bills and groceries and—

She cut me off mid-sentence. "Write it down."

I stared at her. "Write what down?"

"Every charge. For thirty days. Every single one. No rounding, no guessing, no 'approximately.' Just track it."

I rolled my eyes so hard I'm surprised they didn't fall out of my head. I already *knew* where my money went. Rent. Bills. Food. Gas. The usual stuff everyone spends money on. My problem wasn't some mysterious leak—it was that I simply didn't earn enough to cover basic existence. Tracking wasn't going to magically create money that didn't exist.

But Sarah wouldn't let it go. She had this infuriating way of just... waiting. Not arguing, not pushing, just sitting there with this look that said *humor me.* So I figured fine, whatever, I'd prove her wrong. I'd track everything for a month and then show her the spreadsheet and say *see? I told you. It's all just bills. There's nothing to cut.*

Thirty days later, I wanted to throw up.

$340.

That's how much I was hemorrhaging every single month on subscriptions I'd completely forgotten existed. Streaming services I'd signed up for during free trials—you know how it works, "first month free!" and then you forget to cancel and suddenly it's eight months later and you've paid $96 for a service you used exactly once. A gym membership from two apartments ago, still auto-drafting $45 every month even though I hadn't set foot in that gym in over a year. A meal kit service I *thought* I'd canceled—I have a vivid memory of canceling it, clicking through the "are you sure?" screens, the whole thing—but apparently that memory was a lie, because there it was on my statement, $89.99 every single week like clockwork.

A meditation app I'd downloaded during a particularly anxious week and then never opened again. Two different cloud storage plans because I couldn't remember which one had my photos and I was terrified of losing them, so I just... kept both. A wine club I'd joined after one glass too many at a friend's birthday party, where the sales pitch had sounded so good—*curated selections, support small vineyards, you're basically a sommelier now*—and I'd signed up thinking I'd cancel after the first shipment, except the first shipment was pretty good, and then I forgot about it entirely, and now I had three boxes of wine I hadn't ordered sitting in my apartment and $180 gone from my account.

I wasn't bad with money.

I was flying blind. And apparently, so is everyone else.

Here's what nobody tells you about cash flow: it's not actually about the math.

I mean, obviously there's math involved—you can't escape addition and subtraction, sorry—but the *problem* isn't that people don't know how to add up their expenses and compare them to income. The problem is they have no idea what those expenses actually *are*.

Most budgeting advice treats tracking like it's just basic record-keeping. Add up what comes in, subtract what goes out, done. And if the number at the end is negative, well, clearly you're spending too much. Cut back. Easy.

Except it's not easy, because that entire approach rests on an assumption that collapses the moment you're actually living paycheck-to-paycheck: it assumes you already know where every dollar is going. It assumes your expenses are predictable, visible, manageable. It assumes you have enough margin to *absorb* the process of figuring this out—that you're already covering your bills and just need better organization.

But what if you're not? What if the math already doesn't work, and you don't know why? What if your paycheck is already less than your bills and the problem isn't organization—it's that you're in triage mode and don't even realize it because you can't see where the bleeding is coming from?

That's the gap. That's what this chapter is actually about. Not adding and subtracting. Seeing patterns. Knowing which expenses you can control and which ones you can't. Finding the leaks before the whole boat goes down.

And it starts with actually *looking*. Which most of us don't do, because looking is terrifying.

Let me tell you what happens when you don't look.

You live in this constant low-grade panic. It's like white noise in the background of your entire life—you stop noticing it consciously, but it's there, humming, draining you. Every time you swipe your card, there's this half-second of dread: *will it go through?* Sometimes you hold your breath. Sometimes you avoid eye contact with the cashier, like they can see your account balance on your face.

You stop checking your bank balance because you don't want to know. You'll check it later. After this purchase. After payday. After... something. The number is Schrödinger's bank account—as long as you don't look, it could be anything. It could be fine. (It's not fine. You know it's not fine. But not-looking lets you pretend for just a little bit longer.)

You start making decisions based on gut feeling instead of actual information. *Can I afford this?* becomes *Does it feel like I can afford this?* And that feeling is almost always wrong, because feelings are based on vibes and wishful thinking and how much emotional energy you have left after a long day, not on your actual account balance.

So you buy the thing. Or you don't buy the thing, but you beat yourself up about wanting it, which somehow feels worse than just buying it would have. You're making financial decisions in the dark, and every single one is a gamble.

And then the late fees start. You miss a payment—not because you're irresponsible, but because you genuinely forgot that bill was due this week. You thought you'd paid it. Or you meant to pay it. Or you remembered it three days too late. $35 late fee. Then another bill, another late fee. Then your car insurance premium goes up because your credit score dropped because of those late payments, and now the hole is deeper than it was before and you don't even understand how you got here.

You think you're treading water. You're not. You're sinking in slow motion, and the worst part is you think it's your fault.

I'm just bad at this. That's the story. *Everyone else has it figured out and I'm the only one drowning.* So you don't talk about it, because talking about it means admitting you're failing at something that seems so basic, so fundamental. Money management. Adults are supposed to know how to do this. And because you don't talk about it, you don't realize how many other people are in the exact same situation, feeling the exact same shame, convinced they're the only ones who can't keep their head above water.

That's the real cost of flying blind. Not just the money—though that's real, and it adds up faster than you think. It's the *weight*. The constant background anxiety. The decisions you don't make because you can't see clearly enough to make them. The opportunities you miss because you're too busy putting out fires to notice they were there in the first place.

So yeah. Tracking your cash flow matters. Not because it's some boring financial hygiene checkbox you're *supposed* to tick. But because without it, you're just guessing. And guessing costs you everything.

Alright. Let's talk about the mechanics of this, because knowing you need to track and actually knowing *how* to track in a way that helps are two completely different things.

First: we need to break down expenses in a way that actually gives you decision-making power. Most people lump everything together—*I spent $2,400 this month*—and that number is completely useless. It doesn't tell you what you can change. It doesn't tell you where you have leverage. It's just a big intimidating number that makes you feel bad.

So we're splitting expenses into three categories: fixed, variable, and discretionary. I know, I know. Categories sound tedious and bureaucratic and like something a financial advisor would write on a whiteboard while you try not to fall asleep. But stick with me, because this is where the clarity actually starts to come in. This is the difference between drowning in data and having a map.

Fixed expenses are the ones that don't budge month to month. Your rent or mortgage: same amount every time. Your car payment: same. Insurance premiums: same. Student loan payment: same. Phone bill: probably same, unless you're constantly switching plans (and if you are, stop, that's its own problem).

These are the bills that just *are*. You can't wake up one morning and decide to pay less rent because you had a slow week at work. I mean, you *could*, but then you'd be evicted, so let's not. Fixed expenses are locked in. You have to cover them. Period. End of discussion.

The good news: they're predictable. You know they're coming. You know exactly how much. There's no guesswork.

The bad news: they're rigid. You can't adjust them quickly when money gets tight. Sure, you can refinance a loan eventually, or shop around for cheaper insurance, or move to a less expensive apartment when your lease is up. Those are long-term plays. But right now, this month, when you're $200 short and bills are due on Friday? Fixed expenses are fixed. They don't care about your situation.

So step one is knowing what those fixed amounts are. All of them. Write them down. This is your baseline—the absolute minimum you need to cover every single month just to keep the lights on and a roof over your head. Everything else is negotiable, but these? Non-negotiable.

Variable expenses are the ones that change based on usage. Your electric bill: if you run the heat all winter or the AC all summer, it goes up. Turn everything off, freeze or sweat, and it goes down. Water bill: same principle. Gas for your car: the more you drive, the more you spend. Groceries: *technically* variable, though most people hit roughly the same baseline every month for staples, and then it spikes when life gets chaotic and you're grabbing pre-made meals because cooking feels impossible.

Variable expenses aren't out of your control, but they require active management. You *can* lower your electric bill by being mindful—turning off lights, unplugging stuff, not leaving the fridge door open while you stare into it hoping food will materialize that wasn't there thirty seconds ago (I see you). You *can* drive less. Combine trips. Carpool. Walk to the store if it's close enough. You *can* meal-plan to reduce grocery waste and avoid the "oh crap I forgot to buy dinner ingredients so I guess it's takeout again" trap.

But here's the thing, and this is important: variable expenses tend to *track* with your life circumstances in ways that aren't always obvious. If you're working more hours, you're probably driving more—more commutes, more errands squeezed into tight windows—which means more gas. If you're exhausted from working more hours, you're probably less likely to cook, which means more convenience food, which means higher grocery bills even though you're eating less healthy food. (Ironic, right? The cheaper per-meal option requires time and energy you don't have when you're broke, so you end up spending more on worse food. Poverty tax.)

The key with variable expenses is paying attention to the *pattern*, not just the number. Not "How much did I spend on groceries this month?" but "How does my grocery spending change when I'm stressed? When I'm busy? When money is already tight?" Because if you can see the pattern, you can start to intervene *before* it becomes a crisis. You can meal-prep on Sunday when you have energy so you're not relying on willpower and decision-making capacity at 7 PM on a Wednesday when you've been on your feet for nine hours.

Discretionary expenses are everything else. The "wants." Dining out. Entertainment. Hobbies. Streaming subscriptions. New clothes. Coffee shop runs. That thing you bought on Amazon at 11 PM because you couldn't sleep and online shopping felt soothing in the moment, and now it's arriving tomorrow and you don't even remember what it is.

This is where people get defensive. I get it. Nobody wants to hear that their daily latte is the reason they're broke. (Spoiler: it's not. The latte is a *symptom*, not the cause. We'll get to that.) But here's the truth: discretionary spending is the easiest category to cut when money gets tight, and it's also the category where most of us have the least awareness of what we're actually spending.

I'm not saying you should eliminate all discretionary spending. Let me be really clear about that, because the usual advice is "stop buying coffee and you'll be rich!" which is both condescending and mathematically idiotic. Life without *any* enjoyment is miserable, and misery makes it harder to stick to any plan. You need good things. You need moments that feel like living, not just surviving.

But you need to *know* what you're spending. You need to make it a *choice*, not just something that happens to you.

Because here's what I see over and over: people who are convinced they "barely spend anything" on discretionary stuff, and then they track it for a month and realize they're dropping $400 on things they don't even remember buying. Subscriptions they forgot about. Impulse purchases that seemed small at the time—$15 here, $30 there—but add up to hundreds. That's not a character flaw. That's just what happens when you're not looking.

Let me show you what this looks like in practice, because abstract categories are useless without context.

Maria is a freelance graphic designer. Talented—like, really talented, the kind of designer who can look at a mess of a brief and somehow translate it into something clean and beautiful that makes the client feel like a genius for hiring her. But her income is all over the map. Some months she lands a big client and pulls in $3,500, maybe $4,000 if she's hustling. Other months it's crickets. She's lucky to clear $1,800. And she never knows which kind of month it's going to be until she's already halfway through it.

For years—*years*—she felt like she was on a financial rollercoaster. Flush with cash one month, completely panicked the next. She'd tell herself *I just need to be more careful,* but she didn't know what that actually *meant* because she didn't know where the money was going. Being "more careful" when you can't see the problem is like trying to fix a car engine when you don't know what a carburetor is. Good intentions, no traction.

So she tracked it. One full month, every single expense written down. No rounding. No estimates. Just raw data.

Here's what she found:

Fixed expenses: Rent was $1,200—she lived in a one-bedroom in a part of town that was *almost* nice, the kind of place where the building had a name but the elevator broke twice a month. Car payment was $350. Health insurance was $200, because she's freelance so she pays out of pocket and has a high-deductible plan that's basically catastrophic coverage masquerading as real insurance. Phone bill: $70. Car insurance: $110. Student loans: $180, the minimum payment on a balance she'll be paying off until she's sixty. Total fixed: $2,110 per month.

Variable expenses: Utilities averaged around $150—higher in summer when she ran the AC because her apartment faced west and turned into an oven by 3 PM, lower in spring and fall when she could open windows. Gas for her car was about $100 a month—she didn't commute to an office, but she drove to client meetings, coffee shops where she worked because her apartment was too depressing, errands. Groceries were $400, though that number jumped when she was busy and relied more on pre-made stuff instead of cooking from scratch. Total variable: roughly $650 per month.

Discretionary expenses: This is where it got interesting. Dining out was $300—not fancy restaurants, just... eating out instead of cooking. Coffee shops. A pizza when she didn't feel like making dinner. Drinks with friends because she couldn't say no to every invitation without feeling like she was disappearing from her own life. Streaming subscriptions, gym membership, Spotify, a couple of app subscriptions she barely used: $85. Shopping—clothes, home stuff, random Amazon purchases, books, art supplies for personal projects—was another $250. She wasn't buying designer anything. Just... stuff. Stuff that accumulated. Total discretionary: $635 per month.

Add it all up, and Maria's baseline spending was **$3,395 per month**.

Now here's the thing: Maria *usually* earned more than that. When she had a good month, she was fine. Better than fine—she felt like she was doing *great*. She'd go out more, buy nicer groceries, maybe get that thing she'd been eyeing. She felt successful.

But when income dipped below $3,395? That's when the panic set in. And it happened more often than she wanted to admit. Some months she'd invoice a client and they'd pay net-30, which meant the money she'd counted on in March didn't actually hit until April, and suddenly she was $1,500 short with no warning.

The problem wasn't that Maria was spending wildly. It wasn't that she was irresponsible or reckless or bad with money. The problem was that her discretionary spending didn't *adjust* to her fluctuating income. She spent the same $635 on wants whether she earned $3,500 that month or $1,800. And when you're earning $1,800 and spending $3,395, the math just... doesn't work. You overdraft. You put things on credit cards. You panic.

Once she could see the pattern—once she had actual numbers in front of her instead of just a vague sense of dread and failure—she could start making different choices. In slow months, she cut discretionary spending way back. She didn't go out to eat. She paused a couple of subscriptions (you can do that, by the way—most services let you pause instead of cancel, which means you don't lose your settings and preferences). She skipped the impulse Amazon orders. And in good months, she gave herself more room to breathe—but she also started setting aside a chunk of that surplus so the slow months wouldn't hit as hard.

It wasn't magic. It was just information. But information is power, especially when you've been flying blind.

So how do *you* do this? Practically speaking, I mean. Not in theory, but actually.

Step one: Track everything. And I mean *everything*. For at least one month—ideally two or three, so you can see patterns instead of just a snapshot—write down every penny you spend.

I know what you're thinking. *Every penny? That sounds exhausting. I barely have time to breathe and now I'm supposed to log every transaction like some kind of accountant?*

Yeah, it kind of is exhausting. But it's also temporary. You're not going to track every single purchase for the rest of your life. You're doing it now, for a set period, so you can see what's actually happening. Think of it like a diagnostic test. You wouldn't skip a medical test just because it's inconvenient or uncomfortable, right? (Well, okay, maybe you would—I've definitely put off doctor's appointments—but you *shouldn't*, and you know you shouldn't.) Same thing here.

The method doesn't matter. Use an app if that works for you—Mint, YNAB, EveryDollar, whatever. Use a spreadsheet if you like having full control and you're the kind of person who finds spreadsheets soothing instead of panic-inducing. Use a literal notebook and a pen if you're old-school or if apps make your brain shut down. I genuinely don't care. The only thing that matters is that you'll actually *do it*.

I used the notes app on my phone. Low-tech, always with me, no learning curve. Every time I bought something—coffee, gas, groceries, a random Target run where I went in for paper towels and came out with $60 worth of stuff I didn't need—I added a line: *$4.50, coffee.* *$38, gas.* *$61, Target (wtf).* Took me thirty seconds per entry, usually while I was still standing in the parking lot. By the end of the month, I had a complete record. Ugly, disorganized, but complete.

Step two: Categorize. Go through everything you tracked and label each expense as fixed, variable, or discretionary. Be honest. That daily coffee? Discretionary. You don't *need* it, even if it feels like you do, even if it's the only thing that makes your morning commute bearable. I'm not saying don't buy it—I'm saying call it what it is.

Your phone bill? Fixed. Your electric bill? Variable. Your gym membership? Probably discretionary, unless you have a medical condition where regular exercise is actually prescribed and you can't do it any other way. (And before you argue that mental health counts—yes, it does, but also be real with yourself about whether you're actually using the gym or just paying for the idea of using the gym someday.)

Some things are going to feel like a gray area. Is the internet a fixed expense or discretionary? Depends. If you work from home and literally can't do your job without it, it's fixed. If you're paying for the top-tier gigabit plan because you want to stream 4K video and download games instantly, the *upgrade* is discretionary even if the baseline service is fixed.

Don't overthink it. The goal isn't to create a perfect taxonomy of every expense that would hold up in an economics journal. The goal is to give yourself a rough map so you can see where you have wiggle room and where you don't.

Step three: Do the math. Add up each category. How much are you spending on fixed expenses every month? How much on variable? How much on discretionary?

Then—and this is the part that might sting—add up your total income for that same period and subtract your total expenses.

If the number is positive, great. You've got margin. You're covering your bills and you have room left over. (Though if you *feel* broke despite having a positive number, that's a different problem—probably cash flow timing, which we'll get to.)

If the number is negative, you're in the red zone. And now you know by exactly how much. Not "I think I'm short" or "I feel like I'm always behind." You know. $340. $500. Whatever the number is, you know.

And here's where most budgeting advice stops. They tell you to cut back, spend less, tighten your belt. But that advice is useless if you don't know *where* to cut. This is why categorization matters. Because now you can look at your numbers and make informed decisions.

You can say, "Okay, I can't do anything about the $2,110 in fixed expenses right now. Not this month. Maybe not for six months. But I *can* reduce my electric bill by 20 bucks if I'm more careful—unplug stuff, use fans instead of AC when it's borderline, whatever. And I *can* cut discretionary spending by $200 this month if I skip eating out and cancel that subscription I don't use."

You're not just guessing anymore. You're not throwing spaghetti at the wall hoping something sticks. You're making informed decisions based on real data.

Let's talk about variable expenses for a minute, because this is where people often miss opportunities.

Variable expenses *feel* less controllable than they actually are. Your electric bill is what it is, right? You need lights. You need to run the refrigerator unless you want your food to spoil. You need heat in the winter unless you want to freeze. You're not going to sit in the dark wrapped in blankets eating canned food just to save fifteen bucks.

And no, I'm not suggesting you do that. But here's the thing: small adjustments add up in ways that aren't dramatic or miserable.

Take groceries. Let's say you're spending $400 a month, and that feels reasonable—you're not buying organic everything or fancy cuts of meat, just basics. But then you track it more closely and realize that $100 of that $400 is going to pre-packaged meals and convenience food, because by the time you get home from work you're too tired to cook. And another $50 is produce that rots in the bottom of the fridge drawer because you bought it with good intentions—*I'm going to make salads! I'm going to be healthy!*—but never actually used it.

That's $150 a month you could potentially redirect just by planning a little better. Batch-cook on Sunday so you have ready-to-eat meals during the week. (I know, I know, meal prep is its own time investment. But two hours on Sunday when you have energy beats seven panicked decisions at 7 PM when you're exhausted.) Buy only the produce you *know* you'll actually use, based on what you've *actually used* in the past three months, not what you *wish* you would use in some imaginary future where you're a different person.

Or gas. If you're spending $120 a month driving to work, errands, appointments, whatever—could you carpool a couple days a week? Could you combine trips so you're not making four separate runs to the grocery store because you keep forgetting things? Could you work from home one day a week if your job allows it?

I'm not saying any of this is *easy*. Meal planning takes time and energy. Carpooling requires coordination with another human, which is its own kind of work. But when you're $340 short every month and bleeding money in ways you can't see, finding an extra $50 here and $100 there can be the difference between barely scraping by and having a little breathing room.

And the key is this: variable expenses give you *leverage*. You can't control the price of electricity—the utility company sets that rate and you're stuck with it. But you can control how much you use. You can't control the cost of gas—that's set by global oil markets and geopolitics and a thousand things you have zero influence over. But you can control how much you drive. These small levers add up. They're not sexy. Nobody's going to write a viral tweet about how you saved $40 on your electric bill. But when you're in triage mode, $40 matters.

Now let's talk about income, because this is the other half of the cash flow equation, and it's where things get messy when your paycheck isn't consistent.

Most budgeting advice assumes a steady paycheck. Same amount, every two weeks or every month, like clockwork. Direct deposit hits, you pay your bills, you know exactly what's left. Easy.

But a lot of people don't have that. If you're freelance, if you work gig jobs, if your hours fluctuate week to week, if you get tips, if you do side hustles on top of a main job—your income is all over the place. And when your income is all over the place, traditional budgeting advice completely falls apart.

You can't just divide your annual expenses by 12 and call it a monthly budget, because some months you're making $3,000 and some months you're making $1,500, and the bills don't care which kind of month it is. They're due when they're due. Rent doesn't say "oh, you had a slow month? No worries, pay me later."

So we need to think about income differently. Not as a single number, but as a *range*. What's your lowest-earning month in the past six months? What's your highest? What's the average? And then we need to budget based on the *low* end of that range, not the average and definitely not the high end.

I know that sounds depressing. If you average $2,500 a month but your low months are $1,800, budgeting for $1,800 feels like you're planning to fail. But here's the thing: if you budget for the average and then you have a low month, you're screwed. You're short, you're scrambling, you're back in panic mode. Whereas if you budget for the low end, the average months and high months give you *surplus*—money you can save, money you can use to build a buffer, money that makes the whole system less terrifying.

And then—this is important—we need to account for *all* your income, not just the big obvious stuff.

Your main paycheck, obviously. But also: side hustle money. That $40 you made selling old textbooks online. The $75 reimbursement from your job for mileage. The $200 you got from dog-sitting for your neighbor while they were on vacation. The tax refund that hit in March. The birthday money your grandma sent. The $50 you made from that freelance gig you almost turned down because it seemed too small to matter.

People leave money on the table all the time because they don't think of these smaller amounts as "real" income. It's just $30 here, $50 there—not worth tracking, right?

Wrong. $30 here and $50 there is $80. Do that twice a month and it's $160. Over a year, that's almost $2,000 you're ignoring. That's not nothing. That's groceries for four months. That's a start on an emergency fund. That's the buffer that keeps you from overdrafting the next time something unexpected happens.

I'm not saying you should rely on side hustle income to cover your fixed expenses—that's risky, because it's not guaranteed. But you *should* be tracking it and using it strategically. Maybe it goes straight into savings. Maybe it covers variable expenses so your main paycheck can focus on the fixed stuff. Maybe it's your cushion for the months when your main income dips.

The point is: you can't manage what you don't see. And a lot of people have more income than they realize—they're just not capturing it.

Here's where people push back.

They say, "Okay, but tracking every expense sounds obsessive. I don't want to live my life nickel-and-diming every little thing. That sounds miserable. That sounds like the opposite of living."

And I get it. I really do. There's a balance. You don't want to become so fixated on tracking every penny that you lose sight of actually *living*—that you can't enjoy a coffee with a friend without calculating whether it fits the budget, that you're constantly second-guessing every small pleasure, that money stress becomes the only thing you think about.

But here's the thing: tracking doesn't have to be forever. You're not committing to a lifetime of logging every coffee purchase in a spreadsheet. You're committing to *one month*—maybe two or three—so you can see what's actually happening. After that, you'll have a baseline. You'll know your patterns. You'll know where your money goes without thinking about it. And you can ease up.

Think of it like learning to drive. At first, you're hyper-aware of every little thing—where your hands are on the wheel, how hard you're pressing the gas, checking your mirrors every five seconds, trying to remember which pedal is which. It's exhausting. It takes all your concentration.

But after a few weeks, it becomes automatic. You don't think about it anymore. You just... drive. Your brain handles it in the background while you think about other things.

Same with money. Right now, you have no idea where it goes, so you're driving blind. Once you track it for a month or two, you'll develop an intuition. You'll know roughly how much you spend on groceries without logging every item. You'll notice when your discretionary spending is creeping up before it becomes a crisis. You'll catch the patterns.

And honestly? Most people find that tracking is *less* stressful than not tracking, once they get past the initial resistance. Because not knowing is its own kind of torture. The constant low-grade anxiety, the avoiding your bank balance, the dread every time you swipe your card—that's exhausting too. At least tracking gives you information. At least you know what you're dealing with.

Let me tell you about the moment everything clicked for me.

It was a Tuesday. I remember because Tuesdays were always my worst day—furthest from payday in both directions, the day when my account balance was at its lowest, the day when I'd start rationing gas and hoping nothing unexpected came up before Friday.

I'd been tracking for about three weeks at that point. Still annoyed about it, still convinced it was pointless, but I'd committed to Sarah and I'm stubborn so I was going to finish the damn month.

I was sitting in my car in the grocery store parking lot, adding up what I'd just spent—$47 on groceries that were supposed to last the rest of the week—when I noticed something.

This was the *third* grocery trip that week.

I'd gone on Sunday and spent $68. Then again on Wednesday because I'd forgotten stuff. And now Tuesday. Three trips, $180 total, for a week's worth of food.

Normally I would've just felt vaguely bad about it—*I'm spending too much on food, I need to be more careful*—and then done the exact same thing the following week because "more careful" doesn't actually mean anything.

But because I was tracking, I could see the pattern. And the pattern was: I was shopping without a list, buying random stuff that looked good, forgetting half of what I needed, and then going back multiple times to fill in the gaps. Each trip, I'd grab a few extra things—chips, a candy bar, that interesting-looking sauce—because I was already there, and it's only a couple bucks, and I deserved *something* nice, right?

Those "couple bucks" added up to $50 a week. $200 a month. Just in impulse adds and repeat trips.

Once I saw it—once I really *saw* it, not as a moral failing but as a *pattern* I could interrupt—I could fix it. Not by "being more careful," whatever that means. But by making a list on Saturday, shopping once on Sunday, and staying out of the grocery store for the rest of the week.

That one change freed up $200 a month. More, actually, because I also stopped wasting food—when you only shop once a week, you actually use what you buy instead of letting it rot and buying more.

That's what tracking does. It turns vague guilt into specific, actionable information.

So here's what I want you to do. Not someday. Not when you "have time" or when you "feel ready." Now. Today, if possible. This week at the latest.

Start tracking. Pick a method—app, spreadsheet, notebook, whatever. Write down every single thing you spend for the next thirty days. No judgment, no guilt, just data.

At the end of the month, categorize it. Fixed, variable, discretionary. Add it up. Look at the total. Compare it to your income.

And then—this is the part people skip, and it's the most important part—ask yourself: *Where do I actually have control?*

Not "where should I cut back" in some abstract moral sense. But where do the patterns show you have leverage? Where are you spending money on things you forgot you were paying for? Where are you making the same mistake repeatedly because you can't see it? Where could a small change—one list, one carpool day, one canceled subscription—free up meaningful money without making your life significantly worse?

That's your starting point. That's where the actual work begins.

But first, you have to see it.

What are you spending money on that you don't even remember?

Now you know where every dollar went. You've seen the line items, the bleed points, the gaps between what you believed and what actually happened. That clarity is essential—because the next decision is the hardest one you'll make: which bill do you pay first when you can't pay them all?

Chapter 3: The Bill Priority Matrix: What Gets Paid First (and Why)

Eighty-seven dollars. That's the number that cost me my housing. I paid a credit card minimum—$87—three days before rent was due, and when the landlord called on Wednesday, I was $87 short. Not $870. Not $8,700. Eighty-seven dollars was the difference between keeping my apartment and starting the eviction process.

My rent was $950. I had $1,020 in my checking account.

Do the math.

The landlord's secretary called Wednesday: "We show your rent past due. If we don't receive payment by Friday, we'll begin eviction."

I sat on my kitchen floor staring at my phone. That $87 had seemed so small. My credit score would've survived one late payment—maybe twenty points, recovered in months. But an eviction? Seven years on your record. Seven years explaining to every future landlord why they should take a chance on you.

That's when I realized: not all bills are created equal, and the ones that scream loudest aren't always the ones that can hurt you most.

Here's the pushback: "But if I don't pay my credit card, won't my score tank?" Maybe. But your credit card company can't evict you Friday. They can't shut off your heat in January. They can't repossess your car while you're driving to work.

The bill priority matrix isn't about who you *should* pay. It's about who can end your life as you know it *this week*.

Tier 1: Survival Bills Rent or mortgage. Utilities that keep you from freezing or overheating. Car payment if losing the car means losing your job. Non-payment has a countdown clock—and when it hits zero, something catastrophic happens.

Tier 2: Consequence Bills Child support. Court-ordered payments. Tax debt. Anything with criminal penalties or wage garnishment attached. These move with legal force.

Tier 3: Credit & Reputation Bills Credit cards. Medical bills. Personal loans. Store cards. Yes, non-payment dings your credit. Yes, they'll call. But a 600 credit score is survivable. Homelessness isn't.

I know what you're thinking: "I borrowed that money. I owe it." You're not wrong. But the credit card company has a collections department, a legal team, and a playbook for customers who can't pay. Your landlord has an eviction attorney. Which one can you negotiate with from your car?

When I finally paid my rent—I borrowed $80 from my sister—I called the credit card company. Explained the situation. Asked if I could pay half now, half in two weeks. The rep said yes in under a minute. No drama. Because they deal with this every day.

Most triage situations don't last forever. While you're in one, the matrix is simple: keep the roof, keep the heat, keep the car that gets you to work. Everything else waits.

Next time a bill screams at you—past due! final notice! collections!—ask: what's the actual worst-case scenario if I don't pay this first? Not the shame. The actual consequence.

Because the bills that can end you don't always come with the boldest warnings.

The notice was printed on pale yellow paper—why do they always use that sickly color?—and it listed dates, legal codes, and consequences in bloodless bureaucratic language.

You've just learned to prioritize rent over credit card minimums. That goes against everything you were taught. The credit card company is going to call. So is the utility company. And when they do, you have more power in that conversation than you think.

Chapter 4: Negotiating for Breathing Room: Talking to Creditors

You're going to have to call them. The creditors, the utility company, maybe even your landlord. And you're going to have to say the words out loud: 'I can't pay this right now.' Here's why that conversation is less terrifying than you think—and more powerful than you know.

Two weeks. That's how long I had to come up with $1,847 or lose my housing. The notice was printed on pale yellow paper—why do they always use that sickly color?—and it listed dates and legal codes and consequences in bloodless bureaucratic language.

Here's the thing: I'd been paying my bills. Sort of. I'd sent $87 to my credit card company because I'd read somewhere that your credit score was the foundation of your financial life. The minimum was $85. So I paid it, felt virtuous, and then ran out of money before rent came due.

The credit card company wasn't going to call the sheriff or padlock my door. But my landlord would. That yellow paper taught me what no personal finance book had mentioned: debt is bad, but homelessness is worse. Some bills can wait. Some absolutely cannot.

I paid the rent. Borrowed from my sister, picked up two emergency shifts doing inventory at a warehouse, sold my bike. Made it with $23 to spare. The credit card payment bounced—insufficient funds—and I got hit with a $35 fee plus a late charge. My credit score dropped 40 points.

And you know what? I didn't care. Because I still had a roof.

That crisis taught me something else: when you're already underwater, when the math simply doesn't work, avoidance is the worst possible strategy.

Most people think negotiating with creditors is a last resort, something you do when you're circling the drain. I'm telling you it's a necessary skill the moment your income drops below your non-negotiable expenses.

Because here's what nobody mentions: creditors would rather work with you than send you to collections.

Think about the math from their perspective. Collections agencies keep 25-40% of whatever they recover. If a creditor can get even 60% directly from you—even if it takes longer, even if they have to reduce payments—they're ahead. You have more leverage than you think.

Not much. But some.

And in the Red Zone, "some" is everything.

Let me be clear: this isn't about gaming the system or weaseling out of legitimate debts. You borrowed money. You owe it. The question is *how* you keep the lights on and the roof overhead while climbing back out.

You might be thinking, *"If I admit I can't pay, won't that make things worse?"*

No. Silence makes things worse.

Ignoring a creditor triggers an automatic response—late fees, penalty interest, collections referrals, legal action. But calling proactively sends a completely different signal: *This person is facing the problem. They might actually pay us back.*

Creditors are assessing risk. Are you high-risk—evasive, unresponsive, likely to default—or low-risk? Communicative, realistic, temporarily struggling but committed?

Your behavior determines which category you land in. And that determines whether they work with you.

These conversations are uncomfortable. Humiliating, even. But you know what's more humiliating? An eviction on your record. A repossessed car. A shut-off notice when you've got kids in the house and it's 23 degrees outside.

Pride is expensive. Swallow it.

Before you pick up the phone, prepare. This is not a time to wing it.

First: gather your information. Account numbers, current balances, recent statements, income documentation—pay stubs, benefit letters, bank statements. And critically, that Bill Priority Matrix from Chapter 3.

When a creditor asks, "What's your current monthly income?" you need to answer immediately, confidently, with a specific number. Fumbling around reads as someone who doesn't have a handle on their finances. Someone who's probably going to default anyway.

You want to project: I'm struggling, yes, but I'm not chaotic. I know my numbers. I have a plan.

Second: run the numbers on what you can realistically offer. Not what you wish you could offer. Not what seems fair. What you can *actually* sustain right now without defaulting on the four essentials—housing, utilities, food, transportation.

If your rent is $1,200, your car payment is $340, your utilities run $180, and you're bringing in $1,650 after taxes, you've got $70 left for everything else. That credit card payment of $150? Mathematically impossible. You could offer $30. Maybe $50 if you're willing to eat rice and beans for three weeks.

But $150 is fantasy. And offering it will only hurt you when you can't deliver.

A plan you can't keep is worse than no plan at all.

Third: decide what you're asking for before they ask you. Options generally break down like this:

Temporary payment reduction—lower monthly payments for 60-90 days, then resume normal payments. For short-term disruptions: lost job but interviews lined up, medical emergency but back to work now.

Forbearance—pause payments entirely for 30-90 days. Interest usually still accrues, but you get immediate breathing room. Use this when you're waiting for specific money—tax refund, security deposit, unemployment benefits.

Extended payment plan—stretch the debt over a longer period to lower monthly payments. You'll pay more total interest, but your monthly obligation drops. For permanent income reductions.

Settlement—offer a lump sum for less than you owe. Rare, usually only after you're already in collections. Wrecks your credit. Last resort only.

Fee waivers—get late fees or penalties removed as a gesture of good faith. Often the easiest ask, especially if you've been reliable until now.

Know which one makes sense before you call. Come with a proposal.

Let's talk about landlords first. Housing is absolute top priority, and landlords are human beings, not institutions.

That changes the dynamic entirely.

I've negotiated with landlords three times. Twice successfully, once less so. Here's what I learned:

Call *before* rent is due.

Landlords hate surprises. Showing up on the first with a partial payment and a sob story reads as disrespect. Calling a week early and saying, "I need to talk about this month's rent, I'm facing a short-term income problem and I want to work out a plan"?

That reads as responsibility.

Think about it from their perspective. They've got a mortgage on that property. If you call *after* rent is late, they're already stressed, already calculating how long eviction takes. Call early, and they're still in problem-solving mode.

Here's a script that's worked for me:

"Hi [Name], this is [Your Name] from [Address]. I'm calling because I want to be upfront—I've had an unexpected income disruption this month [briefly explain], and I'm concerned about making the full rent payment on time. I take my lease seriously and I don't want this to become a bigger problem, so I wanted to talk about options."

Then pause. Let them respond. Don't fill the silence.

Most of the time, they'll ask: "Okay, what are you thinking?"

This is where you come in with your proposal. Not a vague hope. A specific plan.

"I can pay [specific amount] by [specific date], and I can pay the remaining [amount] by [later date]. Would that work for you?"

Notice the specificity. Not "most of it" or "soon." Exact dollars. Exact dates.

When I called my landlord after that eviction crisis—well, the next time I hit a rough patch, I did it right. I called him on the 22nd and said: "I can pay $1,200 by the first, and the remaining $400 by the 15th when I get my second paycheck. I can also give you access to my work schedule if you want verification."

He said yes immediately. I paid on the 15th exactly like I promised, and three months later when I asked for a reference for a new apartment, he wrote me a glowing one.

Because I'd proven I was someone who kept my word even when things got hard.

Some landlords won't negotiate. Especially corporate landlords with rigid policies. But eviction costs *them* time, money, lost rent during vacancy, legal fees.

A rational landlord would rather have 80% of the rent on time than 0% while they spend two months on eviction proceedings.

You'd be surprised how many landlords are rational.

One more thing: document everything.

If you reach an agreement, send a follow-up email or text summarizing what you discussed. *"Thanks for talking with me today. Just to confirm, I'll pay $1,200 on [date] and $400 on [date]. I really appreciate your willingness to work with me."*

Paper trail. Always. And honestly? It also keeps *you* accountable.

Utility companies are surprisingly flexible. More flexible than you'd expect, mostly because they're regulated and required to offer assistance programs.

Most people don't know this.

I didn't until I had my gas shut off in the middle of January. Came home to a frigid apartment and a note taped to the door. Why? Because I'd ignored three bills and two phone calls, assuming I could deal with it later. That "later" cost me $340 to reconnect, plus the past-due balance, plus a deposit.

If I'd called after the first missed bill, I could have set up a $60/month payment plan and kept the heat on.

Learn from my stupidity.

If you're facing a utility shut-off—or worried you might miss a payment—call and specifically ask about these things:

Payment plans: Spread the past-due balance over 3-6 months. They'll usually let you tack an extra $40-$80 onto your regular bill until you're caught up.

LIHEAP: Low Income Home Energy Assistance Program. Federal program that pays a chunk of your heating or cooling bills if you qualify. Income limits are higher than you'd think. And it's not a loan. It's a grant. Free money.

I had a neighbor, Maria, who got $680 from LIHEAP one winter. Called the utility company, they walked her through the application, and two weeks later her account was credited. She had no idea it existed.

Budget billing: Averages your annual usage into equal monthly payments. You pay $120 every month instead of a brutal $240 heating bill in January when you're already stretched.

Medical exemptions: If someone in your household has a medical condition requiring electricity—oxygen concentrator, refrigerated medications, CPAP, dialysis equipment—shut-offs are often prohibited or severely restricted. You'll need documentation from a doctor, but it's worth it.

Deposit waivers or deferrals: If you're setting up new service and can't afford the deposit (sometimes $200-$300), ask if they'll waive it or let you pay over time. Some companies will waive it entirely if you set up autopay.

The script is simpler than with landlords. You're not negotiating with a person protecting their bottom line. You're navigating a bureaucracy with programs already in place.

Call and say: *"I'm calling about my account. I'm facing a temporary financial hardship and I'm worried about being able to pay my bill. What assistance programs or payment plans do you offer?"*

They'll walk you through options. Take notes. Ask for confirmation numbers. Get everything in writing.

Utilities don't *want* to shut you off. Shut-offs cost them money. If you're proactive, they'll usually work with you.

The cost of avoidance? That's $340 reconnection fees and a freezing apartment.

Credit card companies are tougher. They're less regulated, more profit-driven, and they've got less to lose if you default—they'll just sell your debt to collections and write off the loss.

But they're not insurmountable.

The key is understanding that the first representative you talk to has limited authority. They're following scripts. But their supervisor? The supervisor usually has more flexibility. And the retentions or hardship department? They've got broad authority to keep you from defaulting entirely.

Start with this: *"I'm calling because I'm experiencing a financial hardship and I want to ensure I can continue making payments. Do you have any hardship programs available?"*

Many issuers have formal programs. They just don't advertise them.

These programs might include:

- Temporarily reduced interest rates, sometimes down to 0% for 6-12 months - Reduced minimum payments, maybe 50% of your current minimum - Fee waivers—late fees, over-limit fees, even annual fees - Forbearance, pausing payments for 1-3 months

You'll likely need to provide documentation. Pay stubs showing reduced income. Medical bills. A layoff notice. Be ready.

Here's where people mess up: they get defensive.

The representative asks, "What's your current monthly income?" and they snap back, "Why does that matter? I've been a customer for eight years!"

It matters because they're assessing whether you can realistically pay under a modified plan. They're not judging you. They're filling out a form.

Answer honestly.

If you're bringing in $1,800/month and your total monthly obligations are $2,300, say so. They can do math. If they see you're genuinely underwater and trying to figure out a sustainable plan, they might help.

If the first representative says no—and sometimes they will—ask for a supervisor.

Politely: *"I understand. Is there a supervisor or someone in the hardship department I could speak with?"*

Don't get angry. Don't accuse them of not caring. Just escalate. Sometimes the answer is still no. Sometimes the best they'll offer is barely better than what you've got.

But sometimes you buy real breathing room.

You've bought time. The wolves are at bay—for now. But every month you're still watching money disappear to charges you didn't plan for and can barely remember making.

You bought yourself breathing room—maybe two weeks, maybe a month. That time is a gift, but it won't last unless you use it to find money you didn't know you had. Not by working more hours. By looking at what's already leaving your account, quietly, every month.

Chapter 5: The 'Gap Closer' System: Finding Money You Didn't Know You Had

Pull out your bank statement from the past thirty days. Look at the line items. There's a specific kind of charge that appears three, maybe four times: small, forgettable, utterly routine. You probably can't remember authorizing half of them. That recurring $12.99? That's the bleed.

I spent a year convinced I was "just bad with money." That was my story, anyway—the one I told myself when my account was empty two days before payday, when I was putting groceries on a credit card I couldn't pay off, when I'd lie awake at two in the morning doing that mental math that never quite adds up. Everyone else seemed to have their shit together. I was the one who couldn't make it work on a decent salary, who'd gotten a raise six months earlier and somehow still ended every month broke.

Then a friend—someone who knew I wasn't stupid, just stuck—challenged me to write down every single charge for thirty days. Every one. No rounding, no estimating, no "about forty bucks on coffee this week." Actual numbers. Actual dates.

I thought it was overkill. Honestly, I thought it was the kind of advice people give when they don't understand the problem—like telling someone with clinical depression to just try going for a walk. But I was desperate enough to try anything, so I said yes.

Seventeen days in, I found it.

Not *it* like some magic solution, but *it* like the thing that had been bleeding me dry for months without me noticing: $340 in monthly subscriptions I'd completely forgotten existed. A streaming service I'd signed up for during a free trial and never canceled. A gym membership from two apartments ago that I'd somehow never noticed was still pulling from my account. A meal kit delivery I *thought* I'd canceled but apparently hadn't—turned out "pause subscription" and "cancel subscription" were different buttons, and I'd hit the wrong one. Six months earlier. Which meant I'd spent nearly two grand on meal kits I never received, sent to an address I hadn't lived at since March.

I sat there staring at my laptop screen, and I wasn't just mad—I was *furious*. At the companies, yeah, for making it so easy to sign up and so deliberately hard to cancel. But mostly at myself. Because none of those charges were secret. They were right there on my statements every month, in plain English, with the amounts listed. I just... hadn't looked. Not really.

I'd glance at my balance, see it was lower than I wanted, feel this spike of anxiety like a hand squeezing my chest, and then I'd close the app. Because looking closer felt overwhelming, and honestly? Part of me was scared of what I'd find. Easier to just... not know. To tell myself some vague story about how money was tight this month, I'd do better next month, things would work out somehow.

That's the real cost of not tracking where your money goes. Not the $340—though that absolutely hurt—but the *not knowing*. The constant low-grade panic that hums in the background of everything you do. The sense that you're failing at something everyone else seems to handle just fine, that there's some basic adult skill you never learned and now it's too late to ask. You start believing the problem is *you*, fundamentally, when really the problem is that you're trying to navigate without a map.

Most budgeting advice assumes you've already got the basics covered. It's written for people who have margin—people earning more than their bills, who just need to optimize and organize. "Put ten percent in savings!" Sure, great, let me just find that ten percent lying around. "Build an emergency fund!" With what money? "Invest for retirement!" I can't pay for groceries this week and you want me to think about retirement?

That's all fine advice if you've got ten percent to spare. But what if you don't? What if the math straight-up doesn't work, if your paycheck is already $200 or $400 short of what you owe every single month?

That's not an optimization problem. That's a triage problem. And it needs different tools.

The Gap Closer system is one of those tools. It starts from a premise so simple it sounds almost stupid: before you try to earn more or work harder or take on a side hustle or whatever else the internet tells you broke people should do, look for the leaks. Because if you've got holes in the bucket, pouring in more water just means more waste.

Most people—myself included, before that thirty-day tracking challenge—are leaking money in ways they don't even see. Not because they're irresponsible or careless or bad with money. Because nobody taught them to look. Because the friction of canceling things is deliberately higher than the friction of signing up. Because life gets busy and overwhelming and sometimes you're just trying to survive the week, and checking whether that $8.99 charge is something you're actually using feels like one more thing you don't have the energy for.

Let me be clear about what this isn't. This isn't about deprivation. I'm not going to tell you to stop buying coffee or cancel your Netflix or live on rice and beans until you're financially stable. That advice doesn't work, and honestly? It's condescending. You're not broke because you bought a latte. You're broke because the math doesn't add up, and shaming yourself over small purchases doesn't fix structural problems.

But here's what does help: finding the money you didn't know you had. The subscriptions you forgot about. The bills you're overpaying because you've been with the same company for five years and they've been quietly raising rates while giving new customers better deals. The duplicates and inefficiencies that crept in over time because life got busy and you stopped paying attention. That's what the Gap Closer targets. Not deprivation—*awareness*.

The system has three parts. But first, I need you to do something that might feel uncomfortable.

Pull up your last two or three bank statements. Right now, if you can. Digital is fine. PDF, app, whatever. Don't analyze them yet—just have them open.

I know. I know this already feels like homework, and you're probably thinking you'll do it later, you'll get to it when you have more time, when you're in the right headspace. But here's the thing: you won't. I didn't either, for years. There's always a reason to put it off. So if you're serious about finding that gap money—the money that's leaking out of your life without you noticing—do this part now. Two minutes. Pull up the statements.

Because here's what people don't tell you: most of the money you're losing isn't going to big, dramatic expenses. It's not the emergency car repair or the medical bill or the rent increase, even though those hurt. It's going to small, recurring charges that you authorized once, six months or two years ago, and then completely forgot about. Fifteen bucks here. Twenty bucks there. Forty bucks for something you used twice and then abandoned when life got busy. Individually, they're not worth worrying about—who cares about twelve dollars? Together, though? Together they're the reason you're short at the end of every month and you can't figure out why.

Part One: The Scan

This is the simplest step. Also the one most people skip because it's tedious and kind of embarrassing.

Go through those statements—all of them, two or three months if you've got them—and highlight everything that isn't a major fixed expense. Everything.

What's a major fixed expense? Rent or mortgage. Car payment. Student loan minimums (the amount you *have* to pay, not extra). Utilities that don't vary much month to month—electricity, water, gas, internet. Insurance you can't drop. The stuff you genuinely can't wiggle on in the short term without serious consequences.

Everything else gets highlighted.

And I mean *everything*. Coffee. Streaming services. That app you bought once and used twice. Groceries—yes, even groceries, we'll get to that. Gas. The random Amazon purchase you don't quite remember. Fast food. Vending machines. The twelve-dollar charge from a company whose name you don't recognize—put it on the list anyway, we'll figure it out later. ATM fees. Overdraft fees. Late fees. That thing you bought at Target when you went in for paper towels.

Don't judge anything yet. Don't defend anything. Don't tell yourself stories about why it was necessary or justified. Just make the list.

This is going to feel tedious. It *is* tedious. Do it anyway.

Because what you're doing here isn't just making a list—you're building visibility. You're turning that vague, anxious question of "where does all my money go?" into concrete data you can actually work with. Vague anxiety is paralyzing. Concrete data you can fix.

When I did this the first time, my list ran two full pages. I was horrified. Not because I'd spent the money—I knew I'd spent it, obviously, my account was empty—but because I had *no idea* it was that many individual things. I thought I had maybe ten or fifteen regular expenses outside of rent and bills. You know, the usual stuff: groceries, gas, phone, a couple subscriptions.

Turned out I had forty-three.

Forty-three separate places my money was going every month, and I couldn't have named more than a dozen of them off the top of my head if you'd asked me the day before. There were charges I'd been paying for so long I didn't even see them anymore—they were just part of the landscape, like the hum of the refrigerator. There were charges I genuinely didn't recognize until I googled the company name and went, "Oh. Right. That thing."

And listen, I'm not uniquely bad at this. Everyone I've walked through this process has the same reaction. That moment of seeing it all laid out, every single charge, is visceral. Sometimes people cry. Sometimes they get angry. Sometimes they just go really quiet.

Because you can't unsee it. Once you know, you know.

Part Two: The Triage

Now you've got your list. Two pages, three pages, however long it is. Here's where it gets interesting, and also where most people start lying to themselves.

Divide everything into three categories: Essential, Negotiable, and Eliminatable.

And you need to be honest—genuinely, uncomfortably honest—about what "essential" actually means. Because this is where people get stuck. This is where the whole process falls apart if you're not careful.

Essential doesn't mean "I really like it." It doesn't mean "I use it a lot." It doesn't mean "It makes my life easier" or "I deserve this" or "Everyone has this." Essential means: *genuinely necessary for your well-being or basic functioning, and there is no cheaper alternative that would work just as well*.

Prescription medication? Essential. There's no cheaper version of not having an asthma attack.

Work-related expenses you can't avoid—gas to get to your job if there's no public transit option, work clothes if you have a dress code? Essential.

Your internet connection if you work from home or if it's how you apply for jobs or manage your bills? Probably essential, yeah.

Your gym membership? Not essential. (I know. I can hear the objections already. Hang on.)

Your streaming subscriptions? Not essential.

Coffee from the shop on your way to work? Definitely not essential, even though it feels like it at six in the morning when you haven't slept enough and the day ahead looks impossible without caffeine.

This doesn't mean you're going to *cut* all those things. That's not the point. The point is to stop lying to yourself about what category they belong in. Because once you admit that something is *negotiable* rather than essential, you can start asking better questions: Is there a cheaper version of this? Could I do this differently? What's the actual value I'm getting, and is it worth what I'm paying?

Like the gym membership. Maybe you go three times a week, every week, and it genuinely improves your mental health and your physical health and canceling it would make your life meaningfully worse. Okay. That's real value. But is there a cheaper gym? Could you do bodyweight workouts at home for a few months until you're stable? Could you run outside for free?

Or maybe—and this is what I found when I finally looked at my own gym data—you haven't gone in three months. You signed up with New Year's resolution energy, went twice, felt guilty about not going, and then kept paying because canceling felt like admitting failure.

That's not a gym membership. That's a $35-a-month guilt subscription.

Negotiable is where most of your work is going to happen. These are things you could potentially reduce, replace, or restructure without drastically affecting your quality of life. Maybe you switch to a cheaper phone plan—same phone, lower bill. Maybe you cook three more meals a week at home instead of picking up dinner on the way back from work. Not *every* meal, just three. Maybe you find free alternatives for things you're currently paying for.

Eliminatable is the stuff you straight-up don't need and aren't really using. The subscriptions you forgot about. The service you signed up for with good intentions six months ago and never touched again. That charge for something you can't even identify without googling the company name.

Here's where people usually push back. I'm going to address the three objections I hear most often, because if I don't, you're going to use one of them to talk yourself out of this.

Objection one: "But I *might* use it someday."

Okay. Maybe you will. But right now—right this second—are you using it? Have you used it in the past month? Two months? If the answer is no, you're not paying for a service. You're paying for the *possibility* of using a service, and that's a luxury you can't afford when you're $300 short.

Cancel it. If you desperately need it later, you can sign up again. In the meantime, you get your money back.

Objection two: "It's only fifteen dollars."

Right. And that other thing is only twelve dollars. And that other one is only nine dollars. Add them up. I'll wait.

This is how leaks work. No single charge feels significant enough to matter. But you're not dealing with a single charge—you're dealing with fifteen or twenty small charges that add up to $200, $300, $400 a month. Which is exactly the gap you're trying to close.

Objection three: "I worked hard, I deserve this."

You do. Absolutely. You deserve good things in your life. You deserve comfort and convenience and small pleasures that make the daily grind bearable.

But right now, what you need more than any subscription or convenience purchase is *breathing room*. Financial stability. The ability to cover your bills without panic. The ability to sleep at night without that low-grade dread about money humming in the background.

You can't afford things you're not using. You can't afford fifteen-dollar charges that aren't actively making your life better. And yes, you absolutely deserve good things—but you deserve stability more.

Here's what I tell people: this isn't forever. You're not swearing off anything permanently. Once you're stable, once you've plugged the leaks and built some margin, you can reassess. You can add things back. But right now, you're in triage.

And in triage, you cut what's not essential. Not forever. Just for now.

Part Three: Price Comparison (The Negotiable Column)

This is the step most people skip because it feels like work.

It is work. It's boring, unglamorous, tedious work. It's also where you find serious money—sometimes $50 or $100 a month—for an afternoon of effort.

Go through everything in your Negotiable column and ask: is there a cheaper version of this that still meets my needs?

Not a worse version. Not a version that's going to make your life miserable or compromise something important. A *cheaper* version that does the same job.

Car insurance is a perfect example. When was the last time you shopped around? If the answer is "when I first bought the policy" or "I don't remember," you're almost certainly overpaying. Insurance companies count on inertia—they know most people won't bother switching even when they're getting a bad deal, because switching feels like a hassle.

Spend an hour on a Saturday getting quotes from three other companies. You might save $30 or $40 a month. That's $480 a year. For one hour of work. Show me another job that pays $480 an hour.

Phone plans. When did you sign up for yours? What were you paying then, and what are you paying now? Companies love to quietly raise rates or stop offering promotions you were grandfathered into. Call them. Ask what plans they're currently offering to new customers. There's a very good chance there's a cheaper option that gives you the same service—or close enough that you won't notice the difference.

Same with internet. Renters or homeowners insurance. Even prescriptions—ask your doctor if there's a generic version, or check GoodRx for discount codes. I found a medication I was paying $85 a month for available at a different pharmacy for $22 with a GoodRx coupon. Same exact prescription. Same dosage. The only difference was I had to spend ten minutes on a website.

These are boring, unglamorous tasks that nobody wants to do, which is exactly why they work. Everybody's overpaying on something because they can't be bothered to make the call or do the research.

And yeah, sometimes you do have to actually call. I know. Calling customer service is nobody's idea of a good time. The hold music is bad, the menu options never quite fit your situation, and there's a decent chance you'll get transferred three times before you reach someone who can help.

Do it anyway.

Here's the script that works about nine times out of ten:

"Hi, I've been a customer for [however long], and I'm really happy with your service. But I'm looking at my budget and I need to cut costs. I got a quote from [competitor] that's [amount] lower per month. Is there anything you can do to match that or get close? I'd much rather stay with you if we can work something out."

Polite. Straightforward. Not threatening, not angry, just matter-of-fact. You're a loyal customer, you'd prefer to stay, but you need a better rate.

You'd be amazed how often they come back with a discount. A promotional rate. A plan you didn't know existed that's $20 cheaper than what you're currently on.

Will it work every time? No. Sometimes they'll say there's nothing they can do, and you'll have to decide if you actually want to switch or if you were bluffing. But it's worth trying. Worst case, they say no and you're exactly where you started. Best case, you just cut your bill by twenty or thirty percent for a ten-minute phone call.

I saved $52 a month on car insurance by doing this. One phone call. Three quotes. Fifty-two dollars a month, which is $624 a year, which was the difference between ending the year $800 in the hole and ending it $176 short. Still not great, but a hell of a lot better than where I started.

Let me show you what this looks like in practice, because abstract advice only gets you so far.

Sarah is a single mom in her early thirties, working as a paralegal at a mid-sized firm in Ohio. She's got an eight-year-old daughter, Mia. Her paycheck—after taxes, after health insurance, after the 401(k) contribution she can't really afford but her boss kept pushing so she signed up for three percent just to make him stop—comes out to about $2,800 a month.

Rent is $1,100 for a two-bedroom apartment that's not great but it's in a decent school district, and that matters. Childcare is $650 a month for after-school care because Sarah's shift doesn't end until 5:30 and school lets out at 3:15. Car payment is $280—she bought used, but it's a reliable used, because she can't afford to have it break down when she's got to get Mia to school and herself to work. Insurance is $115. Utilities—electric, water, gas—average about $180, a little higher in winter, a little lower in summer.

Add it up: $2,325 in fixed expenses she can't wiggle on. Which leaves $475 a month for everything else. Food, gas, clothing for a kid who's growing out of shoes every four months, any unexpected costs.

Except she's been coming up short. Not by a huge amount—usually $100 to $150—but short enough that she's been putting groceries on a credit card and then not paying it off, which means interest, which means the hole gets deeper every month.

She felt stuck. She'd tried "budgeting" before, in the sense of downloading an app and writing down what she *should* spend in each category. Groceries: $400. Gas: $120. Misc: $200. It looked reasonable on the screen. Then she'd blow past the grocery number by the second week because Mia needed snacks for the class party and they were out of milk and the chicken she'd planned to cook had gone bad in the fridge because she'd worked late three nights in a row and forgotten about it.

The app would send her a notification: "You're over budget in Groceries." She'd feel like shit, delete the app, and give up.

The problem wasn't that she didn't know what a budget was supposed to look like. The problem was she didn't know where her money was actually *going*.

So she ran the scan. Pulled up three months of bank statements, highlighted everything that wasn't rent, utilities, childcare, car payment, or insurance. When she added it all up, she was spending—on average—about $600 a month on "everything else."

Which was more than the $475 she actually had. Which explained why she kept coming up short.

But it still didn't tell her *where* the money was going. So she broke it down further, line by line, and here's what she found:

Eliminatable:

A gym membership she'd signed up for in January with New Year's resolution energy. She'd gone exactly twice—once for the tour, once the week after she signed up. Then Mia got sick, and work got crazy, and going to the gym at 9 PM after picking Mia up from aftercare and making dinner and helping with homework just felt impossible. But she kept paying. Thirty-five dollars a month, gone.

She didn't even feel bad about canceling it. Mostly she felt stupid for not canceling it sooner.

Negotiable:

Coffee and lunches. This one hurt to look at, because she hadn't thought of it as a category—it was just... life. Survival. She'd grab coffee on the way to work most mornings because making it at home would mean getting up fifteen minutes earlier and she was already exhausted. Four-fifty for a medium latte. Then lunch three or four times a week, because she didn't have time to pack anything the night before and the break room microwave was broken half the time anyway, so she'd run out to the sandwich place down the block. Ten to twelve dollars each time, depending on whether she got a drink.

It didn't *feel* like that much in the moment. A coffee here, a sandwich there. But when she added it up: $180 a month.

That's $2,160 a year. That's a decent used car. That's two months of rent.

Negotiable:

Three streaming subscriptions—Netflix, Hulu, Disney+—totaling $45 a month. Mia watched Disney+ pretty regularly; Sarah had no intention of canceling that one and dealing with the fallout. She watched Netflix maybe once a week, if that, usually falling asleep twenty minutes into whatever she'd put on because she was too tired to actually follow a plot. Hulu she'd signed up for to watch one specific show her coworker had recommended, binged it in a weekend, and then... forgot it existed.

Negotiable:

Target. Oh, Target. Sarah loved Target. Hated Target. Mostly hated how much money she spent there without meaning to.

She'd go in for paper towels and come out with $40 worth of stuff she didn't plan on buying. Candles. Clearance clothes that were cute but didn't quite fit right. A new throw pillow because it was on sale and would look good on the couch. Those little impulse grabs were adding up to about $120 a month—more than her actual grocery bill at the regular store.

Sarah sat with this list for a while. She didn't want to cut everything. She was already stretched thin, already doing everything she could think of to make it work, and the idea of cutting more just made her tired. What she needed was to find $150 a month without making herself miserable. Without feeling like she was depriving herself of every small thing that made life bearable.

Here's what she decided:

Coffee and lunches: She'd brew coffee at home four days a week. Not all five—she decided that Friday morning coffee from the good place down the street was her non-negotiable treat, the thing that made the week feel bearable, the small luxury she wasn't giving up. It mattered to her. So she kept it.

Four days a week, coffee at home. She bought a decent travel mug—$18, one-time cost—and a bag of coffee she actually liked, not the cheapest stuff that tasted like dirt. It took an extra ten minutes in the morning, which meant setting her alarm ten minutes earlier, which sucked. But it saved about $70 a month.

Lunches: She started packing two days a week. Not every day, because that felt overwhelming and she knew she wouldn't stick with it. Just two. Monday and Wednesday. She'd make extra dinner on Sunday and Tuesday nights, pack the leftovers in a container, grab it on her way out the door. It wasn't fancy. Sometimes it was just pasta with butter and whatever vegetables she had lying around. But it was food, and it was free, and it meant she wasn't spending twelve bucks on a mediocre sandwich.

That saved another $80 to $100 a month, depending on the week.

Streaming services: Canceled Hulu immediately. Didn't even hesitate. Saved $15.

Target trips: This was harder, because it wasn't a recurring charge she could just cancel. It was a *habit*. A way of moving through the world. She'd have a hard day at work, need to pick up something—anything—on the way home, and she'd stop at Target because it was on the way and because walking through the aisles felt soothing, like a reset.

So she made a rule: no Target trips unless she had a list written down before she left the house. And no buying anything that wasn't on the list without waiting 24 hours. If she still wanted it the next day, fine. She could go back and get it.

Most of the time, she forgot about it. Or she'd look at the thing on her phone the next day and think, "Why did I even want that?" Impulse spending dropped from $120 a month to about $30.

Total savings: $175 a month.

That's the gap. That's the difference between ending every month in a panic, scrambling to figure out how to cover the shortfall, putting groceries on a credit card she couldn't pay off, and ending every month with a little breathing room. Not a lot—she wasn't suddenly flush with cash. But enough that she stopped waking up at 2 AM doing that mental math that never works out.

Sarah didn't overhaul her entire life. She didn't stop drinking coffee or cancel all her entertainment or never set foot in Target again. She made a few targeted adjustments to things that weren't actually giving her much value.

And here's what she told me a couple months later, after it had stuck: it didn't *feel* like sacrifice. Because the coffee she was giving up wasn't really about the coffee—it was about convenience, about not having to think. Once she set up a routine (coffee maker on a timer so it was ready when she woke up, lunch packed the night before while she was cleaning up from dinner), it took about the same amount of effort. The streaming service she canceled? She genuinely didn't miss it. Couldn't remember the last show she'd watched on it. The Target impulse buys? Half the time she couldn't even remember what she'd bought the week before.

She wasn't giving up things she loved. She was cutting things she didn't even notice.

Let me give you another example, because not everyone's situation looks like Sarah's.

Michael is a freelance graphic designer, thirty-six, living in Austin. His income is all over the place depending on how many clients come through in a given month and how big the projects are. Some months he clears $4,000. Some months it's $2,200. He never quite knows until the invoices get paid, which is its own source of stress.

His fixed expenses—rent for a one-bedroom, car payment, minimum payments on old credit card debt from a rough patch two years ago when work dried up for three months—add up to about $1,800. So in theory, even his worst months should leave him with $400 for food, gas, software subscriptions, and everything else.

In practice? He's constantly broke. Constantly stressed. Constantly wondering where the hell the money went, because it feels like he just got paid and now his account is at $87 and rent is due in four days.

He ran the scan. Three months of statements, every charge highlighted except the big fixed ones. When he added it up, he was spending close to $900 a month on "everything else."

Which meant that in a bad month, he was $500 short. Even in a good month, he wasn't building any cushion, because lifestyle creep is real and when money came in he'd relax a little, order dinner instead of cooking, buy that design resource pack he didn't strictly need but it was on sale.

Here's what the triage revealed:

Essential:

Sixty dollars a month in software subscriptions he genuinely needed for client work—Adobe Creative Cloud, a couple of niche tools for specific kinds of projects. He'd looked into cheaper alternatives. They didn't cut it. This was legitimately non-negotiable.

Negotiable:

A hundred and forty dollars a month eating out. Lunch, mostly, but also breakfast sometimes and dinner when he was too burned out to cook. The pattern was consistent: he'd work through the afternoon, forget to eat, then get starving around 3 PM and order delivery because he didn't have the energy to cook or even drive somewhere. By the time the food arrived—mediocre, lukewarm—he'd have dropped $15 to $18 on a sandwich and fries he didn't even enjoy.

Negotiable:

A premium music streaming subscription. Fifteen bucks a month. He liked having music while he worked—it helped him focus, drowned out the upstairs neighbor's footsteps—but did he need the premium version with offline downloads and high-quality audio and no ads? Not really. The free version would work fine. He just... hadn't thought about it.

Negotiable:

Eighty-five dollars a month across a bunch of app subscriptions. A meditation app he'd used religiously for three weeks in February and then abandoned. A habit tracker that was supposed to help him stay organized. A note-taking tool with way more features than he ever used—he basically treated it like a fancier version of Apple Notes and paid $12 a month for the privilege. A couple of design resource libraries he'd signed up for during a "research phase" for a project that never materialized. He hadn't opened them in three months.

Negotiable:

Impulse design resource purchases. Fonts, icon packs, stock photos, textures. He'd be scrolling through a design site, see something cool, think "I might use this on a project someday," and buy it. It was never much—$8 here, $15 there, $25 for a bundle that was "such a good deal." But it averaged out to about $75 a month, and he could count on one hand the number of things he'd actually used.

Michael's goal was to find $400 a month—enough to cover the gap in his bad months and start building a buffer for the in-between ones. Here's how he got there:

Eating out: He started meal-prepping on Sundays. Nothing fancy—he wasn't suddenly becoming a gourmet chef. Just batch-cooking a big pot of something (chili, stir-fry, pasta with sausage and peppers, whatever) that he could portion out into containers and grab for lunch during the week.

It took about two hours on Sunday afternoon, which he resented at first because Sundays were supposed to be his day off. But it saved him close to $90 a month, and the food was better than the lukewarm sandwiches from delivery. Actually tasted like something.

Music streaming: Downgraded to the basic plan with ads. He'd thought the ads would drive him crazy, but honestly? He barely noticed. Saved $10 a month.

App subscriptions: Went through the list and canceled everything except the note-taking tool, which he actually used every single day and genuinely got value from. Everything else: gone. Saved $70.

Design resources: This one was tricky because it wasn't a subscription he could just cancel—it was a behavior. A reflex. See something cool, buy it, feel like he was investing in his craft.

So he instituted the same 24-hour rule Sarah had used for Target. If he saw something he wanted to buy, he bookmarked it and waited a day. If he still wanted it the next day—and if he could articulate a *specific project* he'd use it for, not just "might be useful someday"—he bought it.

Most of the time, he forgot about it. Or he'd look at it the next day and realize he already owned something similar, or it wasn't actually as cool as he'd thought in the moment. Impulse spending dropped to about $15 a month. Saved $60.

Total: $230 a month.

Not quite the $400 he needed, but close enough that he wasn't in constant crisis mode anymore. And it gave him room to think about the next step—not just plugging leaks, but actually bringing in more money, finding better clients, raising his rates.

But he couldn't have gotten there without closing the gap first. Because when you're $500 short every month, you can't think strategically. You can't plan. You're just scrambling.

Here's the worksheet framework. I'm giving this to you not because I think frameworks are magic, but because having a structure makes it easier to actually *do* the thing instead of just thinking about doing it.

The Gap Closer Worksheet

Step 1: The Scan Pull up your last 2–3 months of bank statements. List every non-essential recurring expense. Be thorough—if you don't recognize a charge, look it up. Write down the amount and how often it hits (monthly, weekly, annual subscription that bills once a year but you forgot about).

Step 2: The Triage Go through your list and mark each item: - **E** (Essential): Truly necessary for your well-being or basic functioning, no cheaper alternative - **N** (Negotiable): Could be reduced, replaced, or restructured without making your life miserable - **X** (Eliminatable): Not using it, forgot about it, or can live without it

Be ruthless. "I like it" doesn't make it essential. "I might use it someday" doesn't make it essential. "It's only fifteen dollars" doesn't make it essential.

Step 3: Eliminate Cancel everything marked X. Do it now—right now, before you close this book—because if you wait you'll talk yourself out of it. Most subscriptions can be canceled online in under two minutes. The ones that make you call? That's deliberate. They're counting on you not wanting to deal with it. Call anyway.

Step 4: Negotiate the Negotiables For everything marked N, pick one of three moves: - **Reduce:** Cut the frequency or amount (eat out less often, downgrade to a cheaper service tier, buy the store brand instead of name brand) - **Replace:** Find a cheaper alternative that meets the same need (switch insurance companies, find a cheaper gym, use the library instead of buying books) - **Restructure:** Change *how* you do the thing (meal prep instead of takeout, brew coffee at home, carpool, use free YouTube workouts instead of paying for a gym)

You don't have to do all three for every item. Just pick the move that makes sense for that particular expense.

Step 5: Price-Compare the Big Ones For major negotiables—car insurance, renters or homeowners insurance, internet, phone plan—get quotes from at least two competitors. Then call your current provider with the best quote you found and ask if they can match it or beat it.

Script: “Hi, I’ve been a customer for [X time], and I’m happy with your service. But I’m looking at my budget and need to cut costs. I got a quote from [competitor] for [amount]. Can you match that or get close? I’d rather stay with you if we can work something out.”

Polite. Direct. Not threatening. You’re giving them a chance to keep you as a customer.

Will it work every time? No. Is it worth ten minutes on the phone to potentially save $40 a month? Absolutely.

Step 6: Track for 30 Days Set a reminder for one month from today. Pull up your statements again and see if the changes stuck. Did you actually cancel the things you meant to cancel, or did some of them slip through? Did any new subscriptions creep in? Have you found any new leaks?

This isn’t a one-time thing. It’s a practice. You’re building the habit of *seeing* where your money goes instead of just letting it happen to you.

Let’s talk about what happens after you’ve done this—after you’ve found that $150 or $200 or $350 a month that was leaking out without you noticing.

First: it’s going to feel weird. Maybe even uncomfortable.

If you’ve been living in constant financial stress for months or years, a little breathing room can actually feel *wrong* at first. Like you're forgetting something. Like the other shoe is about to drop. That's normal. Your nervous system has been in crisis mode for so long that calm feels suspicious.

Give it time. Let yourself adjust to not panicking every time you check your bank balance.

Second: you're going to be tempted to fill the gap back up.

The money you just freed up is going to feel like *extra* money, and extra money is for spending, right? You've been so careful, you've been so disciplined, you deserve to treat yourself.

And yeah, you do. But not yet.

Right now, that gap money has a job: it's your margin. It's the difference between barely scraping by and having room to breathe. Between one unexpected expense throwing you into a spiral and being able to handle it without panic.

Don't spend it just because it's there. Let it sit. Let it do its job, which is giving you stability.

Third—and this is the part that surprised me when I first did this—you're going to start noticing *other* leaks.

Once you've built the habit of actually looking at where your money goes, you'll start seeing patterns you didn't notice before. You'll catch yourself reaching for your wallet and think, "Wait, do I actually need this, or is this just reflex?" You'll see a subscription renewal email and actually read it instead of archiving it automatically.

It's like when you learn a new word and then suddenly you see it everywhere. You didn't change the world—you changed what you're paying attention to.

That's the real power of the Gap Closer. Not the money you save, though that's real and it matters. The shift in how you see money moving through your life. The end of flying blind.

Here's what I wish someone had told me, back when I was staring at that $340 in forgotten subscriptions and feeling like an idiot:

This isn't about being smarter or more disciplined or better with money. It's about having systems that work.

Nobody's brain is designed to track forty-three recurring expenses across six different accounts while also managing a job and a life and everything else. You're not failing because you're bad at this. You're failing because you're trying to do something human brains aren't built for without any tools to help.

The Gap Closer is a tool. It's not magic. It won't fix structural problems—if you're earning $1,800 a month and your rent alone is $1,600, no amount of subscription-canceling is going to solve that. But for most people, there's a gap between what they earn and what they think they're spending. Money disappearing into small charges they can't track, inefficiencies they don't see, things they're paying for that they don't value.

Close that gap, and you buy yourself time. Room to think. Space to figure out the next move instead of just scrambling to survive the week.

You're not going to fix everything in one afternoon. But you can find that first $100, $200, $300. You can see where it's going instead of just wondering where it went.

And once you can see it, you can change it.

The rest of the book builds from here—how to protect that margin you just created, how to build a buffer so one bad month doesn't destroy you, how to think past triage into actual planning. But none of that works if you're still bleeding money in ways you can't see.

So before we go any further: pull up those statements. Make the list. Run the numbers.

Find your $340.

That recurring $12.99 charge? The streaming service you forgot you were paying for? It showed up every month for eleven months—$143 total—before you even noticed it was there.

You found $73 this month. Maybe $140. Those dollars are real—not because you earned more, but because you stopped the bleed. The question is: what do you do with them? The instinct is to spend them immediately on whatever's screaming loudest. Resist that. Those dollars have a different job.

Chapter 6: Building a 'Buffer' Fund: The First Step to Stability

The overdraft notice. Maya's arrived at 9:47 AM in the produce section, three days after payday. Jessica's came at 2 PM on a Thursday, six days after payday. Mine hit at 11:23 PM on a Sunday, while I was brushing my teeth, four days after payday. Different times, different people, same sickening drop in your stomach when the notification banner says your account is negative.

No yellow paper arrived this month. The rent cleared on the first, not the eighth, not the fifteenth. That pale yellow notice that used to haunt your mailbox? It hasn't appeared in sixty days.

Three days. That's how long it had been since her paycheck hit. Three days, and she was already underwater.

She put the apples back. Then she stood there for a minute doing the math in her head—which didn't make sense, because she'd *already* done the math. Monday: paycheck deposited, $1,847 after taxes. Tuesday: groceries, $67. Wednesday: electric bill, $112. Gas, $23 to fill the tank halfway. Thursday morning: $34 overdraft fee because apparently the electric company pulled their payment through a day earlier than she'd budgeted for, and that triggered the overdraft, and now she was standing here with a cart full of food she couldn't afford holding a bunch of bananas wondering what the hell she was supposed to cut.

This is what broke people know that comfortable people don't: it's not the big disasters that kill you. It's the $34 overdraft on a Wednesday morning in the grocery store when you've done everything right and it still isn't enough.

I want to tell you about my friend Sarah, because her situation is the thing that finally made me understand why every piece of standard financial advice falls apart for people in the red zone.

Sarah tracked every dollar. I mean *every* dollar—she had a spreadsheet with categories I didn't even know you could categorize. She'd read the chapter on negotiating bills and called her internet provider and her car insurance company and her credit card issuer, and she'd gotten her monthly obligations down by $140. She'd gone through the Gap Closer exercise and found another $80 in subscriptions she'd forgotten about and shopping patterns she could trim without feeling deprived. She was putting $200 a month toward her credit card debt—real, consistent progress. Six months in, she'd paid down $1,200. The balance had dropped from $6,400 to $5,200, and she could *see* the finish line. Another two years at this rate and she'd be out.

And then her tires went bald. Both front tires. The kind of bald where the guy at the oil change place shows you the tread depth and says "I really can't let you drive out of here on these," and you know he's not upselling you because you can literally see the steel belting starting to show through.

$280.

Two weeks later, her daughter's school sent home a permission slip for the overnight field trip. $45, due Friday.

$45.

Three weeks after that, the tooth she'd been babying along with Tylenol and denial finally abscessed and she ended up in the emergency dentist chair at 7 PM on a Saturday getting a root canal because the pain had gotten so bad she couldn't think.

$1,240. The dentist offered a payment plan: $60 a month for twenty-four months.

Here's what happened to Sarah's debt payoff progress: the $280 went on the credit card because she didn't have $280. The $45 came out of her grocery budget, which meant she ran short on groceries two weeks later, which meant another $50 on the card. The root canal payment plan added $60 a month to a budget that was already maxed, so she had to drop her debt payment from $200 to $140 to make room, which meant her progress slowed by 30%. And then, because she was stressed and exhausted and in pain and she'd been saying no to herself for *months*, she ordered takeout twice in one week because she just couldn't face cooking, and that was another $38 on the card.

Two months after the tire situation, Sarah's credit card balance was $6,800. Not back where she started. *Worse* than where she started. A year of discipline, a year of tracking every dollar and making hard choices and skipping things she wanted, erased. No—worse than erased. She'd gone backward.

When she told me this, sitting in her car in my driveway because she didn't want to cry in front of her kids, what she said was: "I did everything right. I did exactly what I was supposed to do. And it didn't matter."

That's the cost of not having a buffer.

Not the theoretical cost. Not the compound interest calculation some financial advisor could show you on a graph. The real cost: doing everything right and watching yourself slide backward anyway because you have zero margin between your paycheck and the routine chaos of being alive.

The cost of knowing one moderately bad week can undo months of progress.

The cost of that specific sick-stomach feeling every time your phone buzzes, wondering if it's another problem you can't afford to solve.

The cost of standing in a grocery store putting apples back because you're $34 in the hole and you can't even figure out *how*.

Look—I'm not going to feed you therapeutic language about how financial peace of mind is priceless. You're $340 short this month. You need actual solutions, not platitudes about serenity. But I will tell you this, because it's true and because it matters: the emotional toll of living without any margin makes every other financial decision harder. You can't think clearly when you're in constant low-grade panic. Your brain is running on fumes. You make worse choices—not because you're bad with money, but because decision fatigue is real and poverty is *exhausting*. You spend money you shouldn't because you've been white-knuckling it for three weeks straight and you deserve *something*, right? And then you feel guilty, which makes the stress worse, which makes the next impulse purchase more likely, and now you're in a shame spiral on top of being broke.

It's a trap. The only way out is to build some space between you and the edge.

Now. I know what you're thinking, because I've heard it a hundred times: if you're carrying high-interest debt, every single dollar should go toward paying it down. The math is straightforward. A dollar toward a 22% APR credit card saves you 22 cents a year in interest. A dollar sitting in a savings account earning 4% makes you 4 cents. Obviously you attack the debt.

And in a world where you have margin—where your income consistently covers your bills and you're just optimizing the path from "okay" to "good"—sure. Avalanche method, snowball method, whatever gets you motivated. Pay it down as fast as you can.

But that's not your world.

Your world is the one where paycheck doesn't always cover bills. Where an unexpected $150 expense doesn't just sting—it *derails* everything. Where you're not optimizing. You're triaging. And in triage, the rules are different.

Here's what nobody tells you: paying down debt aggressively without any safety net is like trying to patch your roof during a hurricane. Sure, the roof needs fixing. Obviously the roof needs fixing—it's leaking and it's only going to get worse. But if you're up there balancing on wet shingles while the wind is trying to throw you off, you're not actually going to get it fixed. You're just going to fall. And then you'll have a broken roof *and* a broken leg, and both of those problems are now worse than the original problem.

The buffer fund isn't about interest rate math. It's about giving yourself a stable platform to work from.

Let me be specific here, because percentages mean nothing when you're already short.

Let's say you're putting $200 a month toward debt right now. Real money. Real progress. Your balance is going down. You can see it. But you have zero buffer, and your car needs a $180 repair. That repair is going on the credit card. It has to—you don't have $180, and you need the car to get to work. So now you've undone most of a month's progress in one afternoon at the mechanic.

If that happens twice in three months—and it will, because life doesn't happen on a convenient schedule; problems cluster—you've basically erased half a year of debt payments.

Now let's say you temporarily pull back that debt payment to $100 a month and redirect the other $100 into a buffer fund. Yes, your debt goes down slower. For a few months. But when the $180 car repair hits, you pay cash. You pull from the buffer. You don't add to the debt. You keep the progress you've already made.

And critically—this is the part that makes the whole thing work—you don't lose momentum. You don't spend the next two weeks spiraling about how you're never going to get ahead, which is usually when people give up entirely and stop trying.

The buffer isn't about having enough to handle everything. It's about preventing small problems from becoming disasters. It's about buying yourself time to address an issue strategically instead of desperately.

I'm going to give you a target number. You're going to think it's too small to matter.

$500 to $750.

That's it. Not three months of expenses. Not $10,000. Not a "fully funded emergency fund" like every financial book loves to talk about. Just $500 to $750, sitting in an account you don't touch unless something genuinely unexpected happens.

Why that amount? Because it covers most of the things that actually derail people month-to-month. Car repairs. Urgent care co-pays. A broken washing machine. Your kid's school announcing a fee you didn't budget for. The copay for the ER visit when your kid breaks their wrist on the playground. These aren't catastrophic disasters. They're the routine chaos of being alive. And $500 to $750 absorbs most of them without forcing you onto a credit card.

Is it enough for a job loss? No. Is it enough if your car gets totaled? No. But we're not building a fortress here. We're building a first line of defense. Something that handles the everyday shocks so they don't escalate into something worse.

Here's how you do it.

I'm assuming you've already done the work from the earlier chapters—you've found some margin, you've negotiated where you can, you've identified maybe $150 or $200 a month that you've freed up. Some of that is probably going to debt already. Good. Keep some of it there. But not all of it. Not yet.

Let's say you're putting $200 a month toward debt right now. Pull back $100 of that—just for the next three or four months—and redirect it into a separate savings account. If you've freed up $150 a month total, that gives you $250 going into the buffer. If you only found $100 a month, put $75 there and keep $25 on the debt so you're still making some progress and you can see it moving.

The key word there is *separate*.

Do not leave this money in your checking account. It will disappear. I don't care how disciplined you think you are. I don't care if you promise yourself you'll only spend it on emergencies. If it's sitting there looking available, it will get spent. I've watched this happen to people who are *better* with money than I am. It's not about willpower. It's about the fact that your brain does not distinguish between "money in checking earmarked for emergencies" and "money in checking."

Open a basic savings account. Ideally at a different bank from your checking, so there's no instant transfer option and you have to wait a day or two for the money to move. Set up an automatic transfer the day after your paycheck hits. Make it annoying to access. That's the whole point.

Some people like high-yield savings accounts for this, and fine—if you want to earn an extra $2 a month in interest, go ahead. But don't let shopping for the "best" account stop you from just *opening one*. The difference between 4% and 0.5% on $600 is about $20 a year. It's not nothing. But it's also not the thing that's going to change your situation. The *existence* of the buffer is what changes your situation. Start there. Optimize later.

Let me walk you through what this looks like in practice.

Maria is a freelance graphic designer—real person, different name because she asked me not to use her actual name in the book, but this is her real situation. Some months she brings in $3,200. Some months it's $1,100. She's good at what she does, but her client base is small businesses and nonprofits, and they're not always consistent about when they pay her. She's been freelancing for four years. She knows how to manage the income swings at this point, or at least she thought she did.

She had about $4,500 in credit card debt. And she'd been trying to attack it—putting every available dollar toward the balance whenever she had a good month. But her income swings so wildly that she kept getting blindsided. A slow month meant she couldn't cover her full rent, which meant the credit card got used to fill the gap, which meant the debt went back up. Two steps forward, one and a half steps back. Sometimes two steps back.

When we first talked, Maria was adamant that she needed to pay down the debt faster. Every dollar toward savings felt like a dollar wasted, because she could see the interest piling up every month. $87 in interest charges one month. $92 the next. It was eating her alive, and she wanted it *gone*.

And I get that. I do. The math is real. The interest is real. But so is the fact that she'd been "aggressively paying down debt" for fourteen months and the balance had only dropped $800. Because without any buffer, every single slow month or unexpected expense sent her right back to the card.

So here's what we did.

Maria had identified about $150 a month in cuts—stuff she could trim without feeling like she was living on rice and beans. She'd been putting $300 a month toward the debt when she had it, which was about half the time. We dropped the debt payment to $200 and redirected that $100 plus the $150 in savings toward a buffer. $250 a month. Not glamorous. Not fast. But consistent.

Three months later, she had $750.

And then her laptop charger died. The stupid MagSafe charger that costs $85 to replace because Apple has decided that proprietary connectors are the hill they'll die on. Annoying. Frustrating. But not a crisis. She pulled $85 from the buffer, ordered the charger, kept working. The next month, she had a great project come in—$1,400 for a rebrand—and she put $200 back into the buffer to replenish it.

Then a slow month hit. Two clients delayed payments. She was going to be $300 short on rent. In the old pattern, this would've been panic-inducing. Rent is non-negotiable. You can't just not pay rent. So the credit card would've covered it, and the debt would've spiked back up, and she would've spent the next month digging back out.

Instead, she pulled $300 from the buffer and covered the gap.

Here's what changed: her debt actually started going down. Because she wasn't spiking it back up every time life happened. Six months after she started the buffer, her credit card balance was at $3,200—down $1,300 from where we started. Not because she threw more money at it. Because she *stopped adding to it*.

That's the whole game. The buffer doesn't just absorb shocks. It stops the backslide.

Now. Some of you are sitting there thinking: "Okay, but I don't have $250 a month to put toward this. I barely scraped together $80."

Fine. Start with $80.

At that rate, it takes you seven or eight months to get to $500 instead of two or three. That's not ideal. But it's also not a reason to skip it entirely. The difference between zero buffer and $500 is *massive*. The difference between getting there in three months versus seven months is real, but it's not the thing that breaks the system.

And if you're really tight—if you found $40 a month and that's it—then we need to get creative. You've got two levers: cut expenses further, or increase income.

I'm going to be straight with you: cutting expenses has a floor. You can't trim your way to wealth. At some point, there's nothing left to cut. If you've already canceled every subscription, you're buying the store-brand everything, you've negotiated every bill you can negotiate, and you're still only finding $40 a month—then expenses aren't the problem anymore. You're at bedrock. The answer is income.

I know. Easier said than done. But let's be specific here.

You don't need a new career. You don't need to go back to school. You don't need to start a business. You need an extra $100 or $150 a month for a few months to jumpstart this thing. That's it.

$150 a month is $35 a week. Eight hours of work at $12 an hour. Delivered over a month, that's two hours a week. One rideshare shift on a Saturday afternoon. Three grocery delivery batches. Selling stuff you don't use anymore on Facebook Marketplace—I know someone who made $400 in one month selling old kids' clothes and toys and kitchen stuff they'd been meaning to get rid of anyway.

I'm not saying it's easy. I'm not saying you have endless free time and energy to pick up extra work. I'm saying it's possible. And I'm saying it's temporary. You're not doing this forever. You're doing it for three or four months to build the buffer, because the buffer is what creates the space for everything else to work.

Here's the three-month jumpstart version, step by step:

Month 1: Set up the savings account. Automate the transfer. Even if it's $50. Even if it's $30. Get the system running. Track what hits the buffer and what hits your checking. Notice how it feels to see that separate balance grow, even slightly. For most people, this is the first time in years they've seen a number go up instead of down. That feeling matters.

Month 2: You're going to get tempted to pull from the buffer for something that's not really an emergency. A sale on something you want. Your friend's birthday dinner. Ordering pizza because you've been good and you're exhausted and you deserve something easy. Don't. This is the month where you prove to yourself that the buffer is off-limits except for actual unexpected necessary expenses. If you can't hold that line, the whole thing falls apart. The buffer only works if it's there when you need it, and it's only there when you need it if you don't spend it on things you don't need.

Month 3: Hopefully by now you're close to the $500 mark, or at least within sight of it. This is where it starts to shift psychologically. You're not there yet, but you can *see* it. That finish line does something to your brain. It makes the whole thing feel less abstract. And if something does hit this month—if you have to pull from the buffer—don't spiral. Just replenish it next month and keep going. The buffer isn't a one-time thing. It's a system. It gets used and it gets refilled. That's how it works.

One thing I want to address because it comes up every single time: what counts as an emergency?

If your car breaks down and you need it to get to work: emergency.

If your phone dies and you need it for your job or to stay in contact for your kids: emergency.

If you get hit with a medical bill you didn't anticipate: emergency.

If there's a great sale on a coat you've been wanting: not an emergency.

If you're exhausted and want to order takeout instead of cooking: not an emergency.

If your friends are going out and you don't want to miss it: not an emergency.

The line seems obvious when I write it out like that. But in the moment, it gets fuzzy. You'll start rationalizing. "Well, I *need* this coat because winter's coming and my current one has a broken zipper." "I haven't seen my friends in weeks and my mental health is suffering, so this is basically a health expense." "If I don't get this thing now while it's on sale, it'll cost more later, so I'm actually *saving* money."

Stop.

The buffer is for things that are both unexpected *and* necessary. If you saw it coming, it's not unexpected—it should be in your regular budget, even if that means saving $15 a month for three months to afford it. If you could live without it, it's not necessary—it's a want. Wants are fine. I'm not telling you to live like a monk. But wants don't come from the buffer.

Let me tell you what happens when you actually get the buffer in place and then something hits.

A few months after Sarah—my friend from earlier with the tire disaster—finally built her $600 buffer, her washing machine died. Just stopped mid-cycle. Wouldn't turn back on. She tried unplugging it and plugging it back in. She looked up troubleshooting videos on YouTube. She asked her neighbor who's handy with appliances to take a look. Dead. The motor was shot.

In the old pattern, this would've been a disaster. She would've either put a replacement on a credit card (which she didn't have room on anymore), or spent two months dragging laundry to a laundromat and slowly losing her mind, or borrowed money from her sister and felt terrible about it.

Instead, she called a repair guy. He came out the next day. $140 to replace the motor. She logged into her savings account on her phone while he was writing up the invoice, transferred the money to her checking, and paid him. Done. The washing machine worked. Her debt didn't go up. She didn't have to ask anyone for help. She didn't spend three hours at the laundromat every week.

And then—and this is the part that actually matters—she rebuilt the buffer.

The next month, she put her normal $250 into it. The month after that, another $250. Two months later, she was back at $600. The crisis didn't derail her. It didn't erase her progress. It just... happened. And she handled it.

That's what stability looks like. Not never having problems. Having problems and absorbing them without everything falling apart.

Once you hit your initial $500 to $750, you've got a choice. You can stop there and redirect everything back to debt, or you can keep building the buffer up to one month of essential expenses. I'm talking about rent, utilities, minimum debt payments, groceries, gas—the non-negotiables. For most people, that's somewhere between $1,800 and $2,800.

Personally? I think you keep building. Not forever. But until you've got that one-month cushion.

Because $750 handles the small stuff. The car repair. The urgent care copay. The broken appliance. But one month of expenses handles the *big* stuff. A job loss. A major medical issue. Your hours getting cut. A client not paying you for two months because their accounting department is a disaster. Those are the things that don't just sting—they end you if you don't have a runway.

But here's the thing: you don't have to decide that now. Right now, your only job is to get to $500. That's it. Once you're there, you'll have a much better sense of what you need next. Maybe you realize the debt is crushing you and you want to attack it hard for six months. Fine. Do that. Or maybe you realize that the peace of mind from a bigger buffer is worth more to you than faster debt payoff. Also fine. The point is, you'll be making that choice from a position of stability instead of desperation, and that changes everything.

Here's what I need you to hear, and I mean this: this isn't about becoming rich. It's not even about becoming comfortable. It's about buying yourself enough breathing room that you can actually make progress on the bigger stuff without getting knocked back to zero every time something goes wrong.

The buffer is the foundation. Everything else you want to do financially—paying off debt, saving for something meaningful, building actual long-term security—all of it rests on this. You can't build a house on sand. You can't strategize from quicksand.

So start today.

I mean it. Not tomorrow. Not next week when things calm down. Not after your next paycheck. Today.

Open the savings account. Set up the transfer. Put something in it—even if it's $20. Because the first dollar you put into that buffer is the dollar that says you're done letting every random $180 expense define your financial future. The second dollar says you're serious. And by the time you hit $500, you'll have built something that actually protects you instead of just tracking where the damage happened.

I learned this the hard way, which is the only way anyone seems to learn it. Six years ago I was putting every available dollar toward my student loans—$450 a month, sometimes $500 if I picked up extra shifts. I was *so* proud of myself. I was making progress. The balance was going down. And then my car's transmission blew, and I didn't have $1,800, so I took out a personal loan at 16% to cover it, and now I had *two* debts instead of one, and the monthly payment on the personal loan was $230, which meant I could only put $200 toward the student loans, which meant my progress slowed by more than half.

If I'd had even $1,000 in a buffer, I could've covered most of the repair without the loan. I could've put $800 toward it, charged the other $1,000, and paid that off in four months instead of taking on a two-year loan. But I didn't have the buffer, because I was so convinced that every dollar had to go to debt, and I paid for that conviction with two extra years of payments.

So I'm not telling you this from some guru position where I've always made perfect financial decisions. I'm telling you this because I know what it costs to skip this step. And I don't want you to pay that cost.

Once that buffer is sitting there—solid and untouchable except for real emergencies—something shifts. You're not thinking about how to survive this month anymore. You're thinking about what comes next. You stop reacting and you start planning. That shift, from "how do I make it through this week" to "what do I want my money to do for me," is the difference between budgeting as damage control and budgeting as a tool that actually builds the life you want.

But you can't strategize when you're standing on the edge of a cliff with the wind blowing. First, you need solid ground. The buffer is that ground.

And once you're standing on it, once you've absorbed a few hits without falling apart, once you've proven to yourself that you can handle what comes without spiraling—that's when the real work begins. That's when you stop just reacting to your money and start directing it. That's when forecasting stops being a fantasy and becomes a tool you can actually use.

That's where we're headed next.

The buffer is there now. Not much—maybe $200, maybe $300—but it exists. For the first time in months, you have money that isn't already spent before it arrives. That changes something fundamental: you can stop reacting to today's crisis and start looking three weeks ahead.

Chapter 7: Beyond Triage: Forecasting & Proactive Budgeting

When was the last time a bill surprised you? Not the bill itself—you know the electric company charges you every month—but the timing, the amount, the fact that it's due *right now* and you thought you had another week? That's the gap between reactive and predictive budgeting, and it's costing you overdraft fees, late charges, and a constant low-grade panic that never quite goes away.

You don't do the 2 AM math anymore. Not because the money stress is gone, but because you already know what's coming three weeks from now—you forecasted it, you planned for it, and there's no loop of panic to rehearse in the dark.

No context needed. I knew exactly what had happened. She'd gotten her paycheck the Friday before, paid rent, paid the electric bill that was overdue, bought groceries, put gas in the car. Thought she was good. Then Tuesday morning—well, technically very early Tuesday morning when she couldn't sleep—she remembered. Car registration. Due in five days. $187.

The money was gone. Already allocated, already spent, already disappeared into the black hole of keeping her household running for two more weeks until the next paycheck. And now she had this new problem sitting on her chest at three in the morning, and she was doing that math everyone in triage mode knows by heart: What can I skip? What can I push? Who can I borrow from? How bad are the penalties if I just let it go another month?

That text—"forgot about car tabs"—that's triage budgeting in four words.

Here's what I didn't tell her at 2:47 AM, because nobody wants a lecture when they're already spiraling: she hadn't forgotten. Not really. Car registration happens the same month every single year. It's printed on the little sticker on her license plate. The reminder notice came in the mail three weeks earlier. She knew it was coming the same way you know winter's coming—it's not a surprise, it's just inevitable.

But when your brain is locked in two-week cycles, when every paycheck is already spoken for before it arrives, "three weeks from now" might as well be three years from now. Triage mode has no space for future problems. Only right-now problems.

I've been there. I know that specific flavor of 3 AM panic, the one where your body won't let you sleep because it's too busy catastrophizing about $187. And I know what comes after—the exhaustion, the defeat, the voice in your head saying you should have remembered, should have planned better, should have somehow been smarter about money you didn't have.

The shift I'm about to describe isn't complicated. I need to say that up front because the word "forecasting" sounds technical and intimidating, like something people in suits do with spreadsheets at companies that have quarterly earnings reports. What I'm talking about is simpler: looking at next month before next month punches you in the face.

That's it. That's forecasting for broke people.

But—and here's the part that matters—you can't do it while you're drowning. The breathing room has to come first. Which is why if you skipped the buffer chapter, if you don't have even a tiny cushion between you and disaster, stop reading right now. I mean it. Go back to Chapter 6. Build that first $100 or $200. Because trying to plan ahead while you're still in pure survival mode won't help you plan better. It'll just make you feel worse about all the things you can see coming but can't do anything about.

If you've clawed together even a small buffer—even if it's $150 and you think that's pathetic compared to the $1,000 everyone says you're supposed to have—then you're ready. The difference between reacting and preparing isn't having more money. It's having enough stability to lift your eyes from this week and look at next month without your vision going blurry from panic.

Let me show you what I mean with James.

He works at a warehouse, second shift, brings home around $2,100 a month after taxes. Which sounds maybe okay until you subtract rent ($875), utilities ($140), car payment ($285), insurance ($110), groceries ($320), gas ($180), phone ($65). That's $1,975 before we even talk about the credit card minimums or the medical bill payment plan or literally anything else.

So he's got $125 in margin. On a good month. A month where nothing breaks, nobody gets sick, the car doesn't need gas twice because he had to drive to his mom's in an emergency.

For years—years—James lived in this space where December would destroy him. Every single time.

Car registration in December, $180. His daughter's birthday, mid-December, and he's not the kind of dad who shows up with nothing, so minimum $75 for something decent. Heating bill jumps because Michigan winter doesn't negotiate, adds about $90. His workplace does this potluck thing and everyone's supposed to bring something that doesn't scream "I have given up on life," call it $25.

December expenses he could predict with absolute certainty: $370.

Regular month budget margin: $125.

The math didn't work. Never worked. Every December he'd scramble—put some on the credit card, borrow from his mom, skip the heating and wear extra layers until the shutoff notice came. Then January would arrive and he'd be $200-$300 in the hole, playing catch-up through February and March, and then some other predictable thing would hit and he'd be behind again.

I remember him describing it once as "drowning in slow motion." Because he could see December coming. It wasn't a surprise. It came every year at the exact same time like some kind of financial Christmas curse. But seeing it coming didn't help when he had no idea what to do about it except brace for impact.

Here's what nobody tells you about that kind of chronic broke: it's not the individual disasters that break you. It's the repetition. The same predictable thing happening year after year, month after month, and you can't figure out how to stop it. That's what makes you feel stupid. Helpless. Like maybe you're just bad at this, bad at being an adult, bad at the basic task of keeping your financial head above water.

James felt that way. He'd tell me about December coming and his voice would go flat, resigned, like he was talking about bad weather. Just something that happened to him that he had no control over.

Then last September—this is the part that matters—James finally got his buffer up to $400. Took him five months of bleeding $80 here and $90 there from every paycheck, but he did it. And for the first time in maybe five years, he let himself think about December while it was still September.

He looked at the $370. The registration, the birthday, the heating jump, the potluck. All of it predictable. All of it coming. And instead of just bracing for it, he divided $370 by four months.

Came out to $92.50 a month.

So he started setting it aside. Not from the buffer—that was sacred, that was for actual emergencies like the alternator dying or his kid needing urgent care. He opened a separate savings account at his credit union, took ten minutes, completely free. Labeled it "December Fund" in the banking app. Every month September through November, he transferred $95.

By December 1st, he had $285 sitting there.

Still short of the full $370, yeah. I know the math. But here's what $285 covered: car registration and the birthday present. The two things that absolutely could not slide, the two things that kept him up at night in previous Decembers.

The heating bill he called the utility company about—something he'd never had the mental bandwidth to do when he was in pure crisis mode—and got on their budget plan where the bill stays flat year-round. The potluck he downgraded from "impressive homemade something" to "perfectly acceptable store-bought cookies from Costco."

He made it through December without adding a single dollar to his credit card.

First time in five years.

When he told me this in January, his voice cracked a little. Not because $285 is some life-changing amount of money. But because for once—just once—the thing he knew was coming didn't flatten him when it arrived.

That's what forecasting does. That's the whole thing.

Not magic. Not some brilliant financial hack. Just looking at what's coming while there's still time to do something about it, and then doing the smallest possible thing that makes it hurt less.

I know what you're thinking right now. Either "that's obvious" or "I don't have an extra $95 a month to set aside for future problems, I can barely handle this week."

If it's the first one—if this seems too simple to matter—let me ask you something. When's the last time you actually did it? Looked three months out, made a list, divided by the number of paychecks, and started setting money aside before the thing hit? Because most people don't. Not because they're stupid or bad at money, but because when you're broke, looking ahead feels dangerous. Like borrowing trouble. Like jinxing yourself by acknowledging all the ways things could go wrong.

And if it's the second one—if you genuinely don't have $95 to spare—then we're back to the buffer. That has to come first. You can't forecast your way out of a situation where there's literally no margin, no flexibility, no money to redirect. But once you have even $200-$300 in breathing room, this becomes possible. Not easy. Possible.

Some of you have way more complicated situations than predictable annual expenses, though. I know that. Your income isn't steady—maybe freelance, maybe commission, maybe your hours get cut randomly because retail staffing is a nightmare. Or your expenses aren't annual but they're not exactly rare either—medical chaos because your body or your kid's body has decided to be expensive, car repairs on a vehicle that predates the Obama administration, the constant nickel-and-diming of renting from a landlord who considers "maintenance" a suggestion rather than an obligation.

This is where forecasting shifts from precision to scenarios.

Sarah does this. We've been following her since Chapter 1—freelance graphic designer, the one with the $753 monthly gap that she closed through pure triage stubbornness. Her monthly income is all over the map. Some months $3,500. Some months $1,800. She cannot predict which months will be which. Clients pay late, or early, or ghost her entirely and she has to chase them down, or a project she thought would take two weeks takes six and now she's scrambling.

But while she can't predict the specific numbers, she can look at her history and see the range.

So she doesn't build one budget. She builds three.

Good Month ($3,200-$3,500 income): This is when Sarah can cover all her essentials ($2,200), put $300 toward her buffer, and still have $700-$800 for non-essentials and the future stuff she knows is coming. The car insurance six-month premium that's $420. The holiday gifts that aren't optional if she doesn't want to be the aunt who shows up empty-handed. This is when she gets ahead. When she socks money away into those little targeted funds that keep future months from ambushing her.

Average Month ($2,400-$2,800 income): Tight but manageable. Essentials covered. Buffer gets maybe $100 if she's lucky. Future expenses get whatever's left after that, which some months is fifty bucks and some months is literally nothing. She's not going backwards. But she's not building momentum either. Just holding steady, treading water, trying not to slip.

Bad Month ($1,600-$2,000 income): She's in the red before she starts. Essentials alone are $2,200. So she's looking at a $200-$600 shortfall before any variable expenses. This is when she implements what she calls her "bad month protocol"—pause all subscriptions, meal-plan like her life depends on it (because kind of it does), skip anything remotely discretionary, dip into the buffer if she has to.

The key—and Sarah says this is what keeps her sane—is that she knows the protocol before the bad month hits. She's not making panicked decisions at 11 PM while staring at her bank balance wondering which bill she can skip. She's following a plan she wrote when her brain wasn't flooded with adrenaline and cortisol and that specific 11 PM desperation that makes everything feel hopeless.

She reviews her income at the end of each month and tags the next month accordingly: Good, Average, or Bad. Then she knows exactly which spending plan to follow.

Sometimes she's wrong. A month she tagged Average turns out Good because a client paid early. Or a month she thought would be Good turns Bad because two invoices got pushed to the following month. But even being wrong doesn't hurt that much anymore, because she's got the buffer to absorb small miscalculations. The plan flexes. She adjusts. Keeps moving.

The first time Sarah showed me her system, I asked her how long it took to set up. She laughed. "Maybe an hour? And I was being slow and overthinking it."

An hour. To build a framework that handles variable income without requiring her to panic-budget every single month.

Here's what that hour looked like:

She pulled up six months of bank statements and wrote down her income for each month. Saw the range. Divided it into three buckets based on what actually happened, not what she wished would happen. Then she wrote down her essentials—the stuff that has to get paid no matter what. Rent. Utilities. Car. Insurance. Minimum groceries. Came to $2,200.

For each scenario, she did the math. Good month minus essentials = $1,000-$1,300 left over. Average month minus essentials = $200-$600 left over. Bad month minus essentials = $200-$600 short.

Then she made a decision tree. If Good: $300 to buffer until it hits $1,000, then split the rest between future expenses and discretionary. If Average: $100 to buffer, rest to future expenses, discretionary gets whatever's left. If Bad: implement protocol, protect buffer unless absolutely necessary.

That's it. That's the whole system.

She printed it out and taped it to the inside of her kitchen cupboard where she keeps the coffee mugs, so she sees it every morning. Not because she forgets—she's got it memorized at this point—but because seeing it there reminds her she's not flying blind anymore.

I know what some of you are thinking: "Must be nice to have enough income that even the bad months are $1,600."

Sure. Fair. Sarah's broke situation isn't everyone's broke situation. If your numbers are different—if your good month is someone else's disaster month, if $1,600 sounds like a fantasy—the principle still applies. Three scenarios: best case you've actually seen in the last six months, worst case you've actually seen, most likely middle range. Build a plan for each. Adjust as you go.

The income number isn't the point. The structure is. Knowing what you do when things go well versus when they go badly, before you're in the middle of it and your judgment is compromised by fear.

Now let me talk about the thing most budgeting advice completely ignores because it's messy and uncomfortable: the expenses you know are coming but you don't know when or how much.

Your car's going to need repairs. Not maybe—definitely. Just a question of whether it's next month or six months from now, and whether it's a $150 sensor or a $900 transmission thing. Your kid's going to outgrow those shoes, probably soon, and need new ones. The prescription your doctor said you should get filled "when you have a chance" because the thing they're worried about is "probably nothing serious" but you're not totally convinced and it's been three months and the bottle's still sitting unfilled.

Triage budgeting can't handle these. They haven't happened yet. Can't triage something that's still theoretical. So you just... don't think about it. Push it to the back of your mind. Hope it doesn't happen. Or hope that when it does happen, somehow you'll have money, even though you know you won't.

Then it happens and you're blindsided and furious at yourself for not preparing, except how exactly were you supposed to prepare when you didn't know it was coming this month?

Forecasting handles this differently. You create a category called—and I'm serious about this—"Stuff That's Going to Break."

Mark does this. Same guy from earlier chapters, construction worker with variable income. He puts $40 a month into an account he literally labels "Stuff That's Going to Break" in his banking app. Every single month. Whether he feels like he can afford it or not. Some months that $40 hurts. He does it anyway.

Over a year, that's $480. And in the past year, here's what broke:

Phone screen cracked in May. $89 to replace it at one of those mall kiosk places.

Work boots wore through in July. Steel-toe, required for the job site, $110 for new ones.

Toilet in his apartment kept running in September, landlord wouldn't fix it, water bill was getting insane. $35 for the parts at Home Depot, he watched a YouTube video and fixed it himself.

Windshield wiper blades in November. $28.

Can opener died in December. And yes, you can technically live without a can opener, but it's annoying and he eats a lot of canned beans. $15.

Total damage for the year: $277.

He's still got $203 sitting in that account. Which he's not touching. Because something's going to break next year too. And the year after that. Possibly something more expensive than a can opener or wiper blades. The car's got 160,000 miles on it. The phone's two generations old. The apartment's a rental and the landlord's maintenance philosophy is "ignore it until someone threatens legal action."

Here's what Mark told me, and I think this matters: that fund lowered his stress more than his emergency buffer did.

Which sounds backwards at first. The emergency buffer is bigger—he's got it up to $550 now. That should be the thing making him feel secure.

But the emergency buffer is for catastrophic stuff. The engine exploding. Urgent care. The kind of crisis that's scary but also, mercifully, rare.

The "Stuff That's Going to Break" fund is for the constant drip of small-to-medium failures that used to derail him every single month. And those stopped being emergencies. They became... mildly annoying things he had a line item for. The phone screen cracks and instead of panicking, he goes "huh, annoying" and pays for it out of the designated fund and moves on with his day.

That shift—from emergency to nuisance—that's worth more than the dollar amount suggests.

Think about what that does to your nervous system. Every time something breaks—and things break constantly when you're broke, because you can't afford the good version of anything, you buy the cheap thing that'll last six months instead of six years—your body doesn't flood with panic anymore. Your heart rate doesn't spike. You don't immediately start doing that math about what you can skip or who you can borrow from.

The thing is still broken. Still annoying. Still needs to be dealt with. But it's not a crisis. It's just Tuesday.

Mark says he didn't realize how much energy the constant low-level panic was eating until it stopped. Like he'd been running with a 40-pound backpack for years and only noticed the weight when someone finally let him take it off.

Your version of this might look different. Maybe you need a "Medical Chaos" fund because you've got ongoing health stuff and your insurance is a joke with a $5,000 deductible. Maybe it's "Parenting Wildcard" for the endless stream of school fees and forgotten permission slips and last-minute I-need-a-foam-board-for-a-project-due-tomorrow situations. Maybe it's "Old House Entropy" because you're renting a place that's slowly falling apart and the landlord's idea of repairs is sending thoughts and prayers.

The amount doesn't matter as much as the consistency. Even $20 a month, every month, builds to $240 over a year. That's not nothing when you're broke. That's the difference between a broken phone screen being a crisis versus being an annoying afternoon at the mall.

And before someone says "I don't have an extra $20 a month"—I hear you. We'll get to that. But a lot of people who think they don't have it actually do once they look at what's coming and decide the constant ambush is worse than giving up the thing they're currently spending it on.

I'm going to get personal here for a minute. Not because my story is special—it's not, it's the same story thousands of people are living right now—but because I think it matters to know I'm not writing this from some high horse of financial stability, looking down at the broke people and dispensing wisdom I learned from a book.

I spent seven years in triage mode. Seven years of every paycheck already being spent before it hit my account. Seven years of that specific sick feeling when my phone buzzed, wondering if it was another bill I'd forgotten or another fee I didn't budget for. Seven years of juggling, scrambling, borrowing from one month to pay the previous month, robbing Peter to pay Paul and then having to rob Paul next month to pay Peter back.

The worst part wasn't even the money stress, though that was bad enough. It was that my brain never got to rest.

Every decision circled back to money. Every conversation, every quiet moment, every time I let my guard down for five seconds. Can I afford this? What if something breaks? Did I forget a bill? What's due this week? How many days until payday? How many days can I push that payment before they charge a late fee?

I got good at it. Genuinely skilled. I could juggle five financial crises at once, prioritize ruthlessly, make hard calls in real time about what got paid and what could slide another week. I survived.

But surviving isn't the same as living.

I didn't realize how much of my brain the constant vigilance was eating until I finally—finally—had enough buffer that I could look more than two weeks ahead without my vision going dark around the edges.

That's when I started forecasting. Not because I suddenly had extra money. I didn't. My income was the same. My expenses were the same. But I had just enough buffer—$380, I remember the exact number—that I could think about next month without my body immediately flooding with panic.

So I did what James did. I looked at a three-month timeline and saw all the predictable expensive stuff coming. Insurance premium. Car tabs. My partner's birthday. Oil change that was already 2,000 miles overdue. The electric bill that spikes in summer when the AC runs.

And the first thing I felt was overwhelmed. Like I'd opened a door and found ten more problems waiting behind it. Almost closed the spreadsheet right then. Thought about just going back to not looking, because at least when I wasn't looking I didn't have to face how big the gap was.

But then something shifted. I realized those problems were always there. They'd been there the whole time. I'd just been letting them ambush me instead of looking at them head-on.

So I made a list. Divided the total by three months. Came up with a number—$140 a month. Which I absolutely did not have. But at least I knew what I was trying to find.

And here's the thing: when I actually looked at where my money was going, when I tracked it for a month and really paid attention, I found $80. Not $140, but $80. Subscriptions I'd forgotten about. The slightly more expensive brand of something I didn't care about. Five dollars here, twelve dollars there, things that individually seemed too small to matter but added up to real money.

I redirected that $80 into a separate account labeled "Next 3 Months." Every month. For three months.

By the time the insurance premium hit, I had $240. Not enough to cover everything—I still had to make choices, still had to prioritize—but enough to cover the insurance and the car tabs. The two things that absolutely could not slide without consequences I couldn't afford.

The birthday present I downgraded. The oil change I did myself with a YouTube tutorial and $25 worth of supplies instead of paying $60 at the quick-lube place. The summer electric bill I negotiated by calling the power company and asking if they had any programs for people who were struggling—turned out they did, knocked $30 off that month.

Still came up short. Still had to make compromises. But for the first time in seven years, I wasn't reacting. I was executing a plan I'd made when I had the mental space to think clearly.

That felt different. Felt like maybe I wasn't completely helpless after all.

The second three-month cycle was easier. I knew what I was looking for. Found another $40 by switching my phone plan to a cheaper carrier—same network, half the price, took twenty minutes online. Started meal-planning more carefully and got my grocery bill down by $50 without eating significantly worse. Suddenly I had $170 a month to work with instead of $80.

Third cycle, I hit $140. Covered everything on my list without having to scramble or borrow or put anything on the credit card.

Fourth cycle, I had money left over.

I'm not going to tell you that solved all my problems or that I'm financially comfortable now or any of that aspirational nonsense. I'm still broke by most people's standards. I still can't afford a lot of things I wish I could. I still have months where something unexpected happens and I'm back to scrambling.

But I'm not drowning anymore. I can see what's coming. I can make plans that actually work instead of plans that fall apart the moment reality shows up. My brain gets to rest sometimes.

That's worth more than the dollar amounts suggest.

Here's what forecasting actually looks like when you're broke and just starting:

Week 1: Sit down with your calendar and your bank statements. Look three months out. Write down every single thing you know is coming that costs money. Annual stuff. Seasonal stuff. Birthdays. Bills that vary but are predictable. Everything.

Don't panic about the total yet. Just make the list.

Week 2: Add up the list. Divide by the number of paychecks between now and the furthest-out thing on your list. That's your target number.

If that number is bigger than your current margin—and it probably is—don't quit. Just acknowledge the gap. We're going to close it.

Week 3: Track everything you spend for one week. Everything. Not to judge yourself, not to feel bad, just to see where it's actually going. Most people are shocked by this. Not because they're spending huge amounts on any one thing, but because the small stuff adds up to more than they realized.

Week 4: Look at your spending and ask: What can I redirect? Not cut forever. Not deprive myself of everything that makes life bearable. Just redirect from right now to next month.

Maybe it's $30. Maybe it's $70. Whatever you find, start setting it aside. Every paycheck. Same amount. Into a separate account if you can, or a separate category in your budget app, or even a literal envelope in your drawer labeled with what it's for.

Month 2 and beyond: Keep going. Some months you'll find more to redirect. Some months you won't. Some months you'll have to dip into the fund earlier than planned because something came up. That's fine. The whole point isn't perfection. It's having something there instead of nothing.

And here's the thing nobody tells you: the first time you pay for something out of money you set aside specifically for it—even if it's just $40 toward a $200 expense—your brain does something different. Instead of "oh god I'm broke again," it goes "oh, I planned for this."

That's not a small thing. That's the difference between chaos and control. Between being a victim of your circumstances and being someone who's actively managing a hard situation as best you can.

I want to address something before we close this out, because I know some of you are sitting there thinking: "This all sounds great if you've got margin to redirect. But I genuinely don't. I'm not exaggerating when I say every dollar is spoken for. There is no money to find."

If that's you, I believe you. I've been there too. There are situations where the math genuinely doesn't work, where income is less than minimum expenses and no amount of planning or forecasting can fix that.

If that's your situation right now, forecasting might not be the tool you need yet. The tool you need is Chapter 8—the income side, not the expense side. Because you can't budget your way out of genuinely not having enough money. Eventually you hit a floor.

But—and this is important—even if you can't act on forecasting right now, understanding it matters. Because circumstances change. Income goes up. Expenses go down. Debts get paid off. Kids get older and need less childcare. Whatever's keeping you in crisis mode right now won't last forever, even though I know it feels like it will.

And when things shift—when you finally get that raise, or the car gets paid off, or the debt settlement finally clears—you'll be ready. Won't have to start from scratch trying to figure out how to manage the new margin. You'll already know.

That's what the next chapter is about: creating more margin when redirecting expenses isn't enough. But for those of you who do have some flexibility, even tiny amounts—start there. Three months out. Make the list. Find what you can. Set it aside.

The ambush you prevent tomorrow starts with the twenty dollars you redirect today.

I know what some of you are thinking right now. "This sounds great in theory, but I've tried planning ahead before. I make the list, I find the money, I set it aside—and then something else comes up and I have to use it. Every single time."

I hear you. And you're not wrong.

That's going to happen. Probably more than once. You're going to forecast that your car registration is due in July, set aside forty dollars in April, and then in May your kid's going to need emergency dental work and that forty dollars is going to disappear. I'm not going to lie to you and say that won't happen, because it will.

But here's what I need you to understand: that's still a win.

You know why? Because you had forty dollars available when the emergency happened. Forty dollars you wouldn't have had if you'd been spending every penny as it came in. Did it go toward what you planned? No. Did it keep you from being completely underwater when your kid needed a dentist? Yes.

That's what building margin looks like in the early stages. It's messy. It's imperfect. You're not going to nail it the first time, or the fifth time, or maybe even the twentieth time. But every single time you set something aside—even if you end up using it for something different than you planned—you're training yourself to live one step ahead instead of one step behind.

And eventually, if you keep at it, you'll start to notice something.

You'll have a month where you forecasted three things, set money aside for all three, and only two of them happened. And suddenly you've got this weird, unfamiliar feeling: you have money left over that you don't immediately need to spend on something urgent.

That's the turning point. That's when this stops being a desperate scramble and starts being an actual system.

But you've got to survive the messy middle to get there. And the messy middle requires you to do something that feels completely counterintuitive when you're broke: you've got to separate your forecast accuracy from your sense of whether this is working.

Most people quit forecasting because they think, "I'm bad at this. I keep getting it wrong. This doesn't work for me."

But forecasting isn't about being psychic. It's not about predicting the future with perfect accuracy. It's about creating a habit of looking ahead and making decisions based on what's probably coming instead of only what's happening right now.

You're going to get it wrong sometimes. You're going to forget expenses. You're going to underestimate costs. You're going to have things pop up that weren't even on your radar. That's not failure. That's data.

Every time you miss something, you learn. Next time you forecast, that thing goes on the list. Every time you underestimate a cost, you adjust your number up. Every time you discover a pattern—like your utility bills always spike in the summer, or your kids always need new clothes right before school pictures—you build that into your forecast.

This is not a one-and-done exercise. This is a practice. A muscle you're building. And like any muscle, it's weak and uncoordinated at first. You're going to stumble. That's fine. You get back up and keep going.

Here's what I want you to do differently than most people who try this and quit.

Don't just make the list. Track what actually happens.

Keep your forecast somewhere you can see it—piece of paper on the fridge, note in your phone, whatever works for you. And when the thing you forecasted actually comes up, mark it. Put a check next to it. Write down what it actually cost versus what you thought it would cost.

And when something happens that you didn't forecast, add it to the list anyway. Right there in the moment. Write it down with a star next to it or circle it or whatever reminds you: this was a miss. I didn't see this coming. Now I know.

Because three months from now, when you're making your next forecast, you're going to look back at that list. And you're going to remember. The thing that blindsided you this quarter is going into the forecast next quarter. Your accuracy is going to get better, not because you got smarter, but because you paid attention.

And gradually—so gradually you almost won't notice it happening—the crises are going to spread out. Instead of something urgent every single week, it'll be every other week. Then twice a month. Then once a month. And eventually, you'll have whole months where nothing catches you off guard, because you saw it coming and you were ready.

That's the point where forecasting stops feeling like extra work and starts feeling like breathing. You don't have to force yourself to do it. You just do it, because the alternative—going back to constant crisis mode—feels unbearable now that you know what it's like to live without it.

But I'm going to be honest with you about something else.

There are going to be people in your life who don't get this. Who are going to look at you setting aside twelve dollars for a birthday gift in two months and think you're being ridiculous. Who are going to say, "It's only twelve dollars, just deal with it when it happens," because they've never had to choose between a birthday gift and keeping the lights on.

Those people don't live in your reality. And you don't owe them an explanation.

You're not being cheap. You're not being obsessive. You're not being paranoid. You're being strategic. You're playing the long game in a situation where most people can only see the next seventy-two hours. That takes discipline most people will never understand because they've never had to develop it.

So when someone makes a comment, or gives you a look, or tries to pressure you into spending money you've already allocated for something else—remember that their financial margin is not your financial margin. Their cushion is not your cushion. They get to make different choices because they're playing a different game.

You're playing the game where twelve dollars matters. Where forecasting three months out is the difference between surviving and drowning. Where being ready for the predictable stuff means you might actually have a shot at handling the unpredictable stuff.

That game requires you to think differently than people who've never played it. And that's fine. Let them think you're overthinking it.

You'll be the one who isn't scrambling when the bill comes due.

You're forecasting now. You see the car tabs coming in April, the annual insurance bill in July. You're not surprised anymore. But forecasting only works if there's money to allocate, and if your baseline income can't cover baseline expenses, you've hit a ceiling. The only way through is up.

Chapter 8: The 'Income Boost' Strategy: Increasing Your Earning Potential

You've done everything they told you to do. You cut cable. You switched to the cheapest phone plan. You buy store-brand everything, make coffee at home, haven't eaten out in two months. And the math still doesn't work. You're still $280 short this month. That's not a budgeting problem. That's an income problem. And it requires a different solution entirely.

And still, the math doesn't work.

Still $280 short this month.

She runs the numbers again. Moves money around on paper—rob Peter to pay Paul, as her grandmother used to say. Maybe she could push the electric bill to next month? But she did that last month, and now the late fee is stacking. Maybe skip the car insurance payment? Except she needs the car to get to work, and if she gets pulled over driving uninsured, that's a $500 ticket she definitely can't afford. Maybe...

There is no maybe. She's out of maybes.

That's when it hits her: You can't budget your way out of a paycheck that doesn't cover your bills.

Here's what that realization actually costs, the part nobody talks about.

It's not just the $280. It's the three months before this moment—three months of Jessica waking up at 5:30 AM to clip coupons, comparing unit prices on toilet paper, walking past the office coffee pot to drink the stale break room coffee instead, all while her coworker Sarah buys a $6 latte every single morning without thinking about it. Three months of Jessica's brain running budget calculations in the background of every single moment. At the grocery store. At her kid's school event. At dinner with friends where she orders the cheapest thing on the menu and says she's not that hungry.

It's the cumulative weight of small humiliations. The "I can't" responses piling up. Can you chip in for the group gift? I can't. Want to grab drinks after work? I can't. Your daughter's field trip is $35. I can't, but here's $20, is that okay?

It's watching your friends plan a weekend camping trip—not an expensive trip, just gas money and some groceries—and knowing you can't even afford that. Not because you're reckless or lazy or bad with money. Because the money isn't there.

And it's the corrosive, exhausting thought that creeps in around month four or five of this: *Is this just my life now? Is this it?*

Most people waste months, sometimes years, in that space. Trying to trim their way to financial stability when the real issue isn't spending, it's earning. They're trying to squeeze water from a stone. And I'm not saying cutting expenses is useless—we covered that in earlier chapters, it matters. But there's a ceiling to what cutting can do. Once you've eliminated cable, downgraded your phone plan, switched to store brands, and you're still short? You've hit it.

The only math that changes the equation is more money coming in.

I know what you're thinking—this is supposed to be the chapter about *boosting* income, not dwelling on the problem. And you're right, we're getting there. But that moment of realization matters because it's the moment most people avoid. They keep cutting and cutting and cutting because *cutting feels like control*. Cutting is something you can do right now, today, without asking anyone for anything. Cutting doesn't require you to put yourself out there or risk rejection or learn something new.

Increasing your income? That's vulnerable. That's uncomfortable. That requires you to believe you might be worth more than you're currently getting paid, which is a surprisingly hard thing to believe when you've been broke for long enough.

But here's the thing nobody tells you: the biggest income boosts often don't come from working *more* hours. They come from working *different* hours, or changing what you're paid for the hours you're already working, or—and this is the part that surprises people—just asking for what you're already worth.

Let me start there. Because it's the fastest path to more money and the one most people are terrified to touch.

Your current job probably isn't paying you what you're worth.

I don't mean that as some motivational-poster platitude. I mean it as a statistical likelihood. Most companies pay people based on what they were hired at, plus incremental raises that barely keep pace with inflation—if you're lucky. They don't proactively re-evaluate whether your current responsibilities match your current salary. That's *your* job. And if you haven't asked for a raise in the past two years, you're probably leaving money on the table.

I know—asking feels terrifying. It triggers every anxiety about appearing greedy, ungrateful, presumptuous. What if they say no? What if they're annoyed you even asked? What if it makes things awkward, and now they're watching you, waiting for you to screw up so they have a reason to say you weren't worth it after all?

Here's what I wish someone had told me earlier, back when I was working at a marketing agency making $38,000 a year while doing the work of someone making $52,000. (I know this because I eventually saw the job posting when my coworker quit, and that's what they listed the salary range as. For the exact work I was already doing. Yeah.)

Your employer already knows what you're worth. They have a budget line for your role. They've seen what you produce. If you're good at your job—if you show up, do the work, solve problems without creating new ones—they *want* to keep you. Because replacing you costs money. A lot of it. Recruiting fees, interviewing time, onboarding, training a new person to the point where they're as effective as you are right now—that's expensive and disruptive and annoying.

Most estimates put the cost of replacing an employee at somewhere between 50-200% of their annual salary, depending on the role. So if you're making $45,000 and you ask for a $5,000 raise, and they say no, and you leave, they're not saving money. They're spending way more to replace you.

So when you ask for a raise, you're not asking for charity. You're giving them the opportunity to keep a known quantity instead of gambling on an unknown one.

But—and this is critical—you can't walk in and just say "I'd like more money." You need to make a case. And that case needs to be specific.

Start by documenting what you've actually accomplished. Not what your job description says you do—what you've *done*. Did you take on responsibilities that weren't originally part of your role? Train new employees? Solve a recurring problem that was eating up everyone's time? Handle a difficult client situation that could've gone sideways?

Write it all down. Be specific. Use numbers wherever possible, real numbers, specific dollar amounts or percentages or hours saved.

Instead of "I improved customer service," write "I reduced average response time from 48 hours to 18 hours, and our customer satisfaction scores went up 12 points in Q2." Instead of "I helped with the website redesign," write "I coordinated the website migration, which was completed two weeks ahead of schedule and came in $3,000 under budget."

You're building a brag sheet. It feels weird at first—most of us aren't taught to advocate for ourselves like this. Women especially. We're taught that good work speaks for itself, that if you just keep your head down and work hard, people will notice and reward you accordingly.

They won't.

I'm not saying they're malicious. I'm saying they're busy. They're not tracking your accomplishments. You are.

Next, research what people in your role typically earn. Glassdoor, Payscale, Salary.com—these sites aren't perfect, but they give you a ballpark. If you're in a mid-sized city making $42,000 as a marketing coordinator and the data shows that role typically pays $48,000 to

$54,000 in your area, you now have context. You're not pulling a number out of thin air when you ask for $50,000. You're aligning with market rate.

Then you script it. Yes, actually script it. Write out what you're going to say, practice it out loud until it doesn't sound rehearsed, and then schedule a meeting with your manager.

Don't ambush them. Don't catch them in the hallway and blurt it out. Send an email: "I'd like to schedule 20 minutes to discuss my role and compensation. Do you have time this week?" Professional. Clear.

Here's how that conversation might go:

"Thanks for meeting with me. I wanted to talk about my role and compensation. Over the past year, I've taken on several new responsibilities—specifically, I've been managing the client onboarding process, which used to be split between three people, and I've trained four new hires. I've also reduced our customer response time by 30 hours per week, which has directly improved our satisfaction scores. Based on my research into industry standards for this role in our area, and considering the value I'm bringing to the team, I'd like to discuss adjusting my salary to $50,000."

Notice what you didn't do: You didn't apologize. You didn't hedge. You didn't say "I was wondering if maybe possibly..." You stated your case clearly and asked directly.

Now, they might say yes. Great—you just gave yourself a raise without changing jobs or adding a side hustle. If you're making $42,000 and you bump to $50,000, that's an extra $667 a month. That's not just closing Jessica's $280 gap. That's closing the gap *and* starting to build a buffer.

They might say no. If they do, ask why. Specifically. Is it a budget issue? Is there something they need to see from you first? Don't accept vague responses.

If it's a budget issue, ask when would be a better time to revisit the conversation—and get that in writing if possible, even if it's just a follow-up email. "Thanks for the conversation. I understand budget is tight right now. You mentioned we could revisit this in six months—I'll put it on my calendar for March and we can discuss then."

If it's performance-based, ask for specific benchmarks. "What would I need to accomplish in the next six months to earn a raise to $50,000?" Then document that conversation. Send a follow-up email summarizing what they said. "Just to confirm: you mentioned that if I [specific goal], we can revisit compensation. I'll focus on that and let's touch base in June."

And if they say no without a clear path to yes? Or if you hit those benchmarks and they still won't budge? Well, now you know. You're working for someone who doesn't value you appropriately. That's useful information. It might be time to start looking elsewhere.

I'm not saying quit your job tomorrow. I'm saying don't let loyalty trap you in a position that's underpaying you. Companies don't reward loyalty the way they used to. The days of working somewhere for 30 years and getting a pension are mostly gone. People who stay at the same company for years often see 2-3% annual raises, which doesn't even keep up with inflation. People who switch jobs strategically can see 10-20% bumps. That's not disloyalty—that's recognizing your market value and going where it's compensated.

But let's say leaving isn't realistic right now. Or you did ask for a raise and got it but you're still short. That's where side income comes in.

And here's where people usually make their first mistake: they chase the highest-paying opportunity instead of the most *sustainable* one.

Someone tells them you can make $25 an hour driving for Uber, so they sign up, spend three nights a week driving until midnight, and burn out within a month because they're exhausted and they hate it and their car is racking up miles they can't afford to maintain. Or they see an ad promising $5,000 a month doing freelance graphic design—ignoring that the person making $5,000 a month has been doing it for three years and has an established client base—so they buy a $500 course, spend weeks learning Adobe Illustrator, and realize they hate designing and have no idea how to get clients.

They're optimizing for maximum theoretical income instead of maximum realistic fit.

Here's a better framework. I call it the Skill-Time-Profit filter, and it's deliberately simple because if it's complicated, you won't use it.

Get a piece of paper. Draw three columns: Skill, Time, Profit.

Under Skill, list things you're already decent at or genuinely enjoy learning. Not things you *wish* you were good at. Not things that sound impressive. Things you've actually done and gotten positive feedback on. Writing. Organizing. Explaining tech stuff to non-tech people. Baking. Fixing things. Teaching kids. Listening (actually—people pay for therapy, coaching, tutoring, all of which are fundamentally about listening well). Whatever.

Under Time, be brutally honest about how many hours per week you can actually commit without wrecking your health, your primary job, or your relationships. If you're already working 40 hours, commuting 10, and parenting the rest of the time, you don't have 20 hours a week for a side hustle. You have maybe 5. Maybe. And some weeks you won't even have that.

Under Profit, research what those skills can realistically earn in the time you actually have. If you have 5 hours a week and you're thinking about freelance writing, look up what beginner writers charge. Probably $25-$50 per article to start. If you can write one article in 2-3 hours, that's $50-$100 per week, $200-$400 per month. Is that enough to make a difference?

For Jessica sitting at her kitchen table $280 short—yes, actually. That covers the gap and then some.

The highest score wins—but the highest score based on *your* reality, not someone else's income report from a business they've been running for five years.

Take Carlos. He worked in IT support, made $48,000 a year, and was consistently $200-$300 short each month because of student loans and a car payment that didn't leave much room for groceries. He was good at troubleshooting tech problems—that was literally his job—but he hated the idea of doing more of it after hours. What he actually enjoyed was cooking. His friends constantly asked for his recipes. Someone once offered to pay him to teach them how to make his grandmother's tamales, and he laughed it off, but the offer stuck with him.

So he started teaching cooking classes. Not a full catering business—just small groups of 4-5 people in his apartment kitchen, once or twice a month, $40 per person. It took him maybe 6 hours total per session—shopping, prep, the class itself, cleanup. That's $160-$200 for one Saturday afternoon. He did it twice a month and cleared an extra $300-$400.

Was it the most lucrative thing he could've done with those hours? Probably not. Could he have made more doing freelance IT consulting at $75 an hour? Maybe, if he could find clients, which isn't guaranteed. But would he have sustained it? No. Because he would've hated it, burned out within two months, and quit.

The cooking classes he actually enjoyed. People left happy. They'd hug him on the way out and tell him it was the best Saturday they'd had in months. He got to share something he loved, something his grandmother taught him. And it covered his monthly shortfall with enough left over to start putting $50-$100 into savings.

That's what I mean by sustainable. It's not just about the money per hour. It's about whether you can actually keep doing it without starting to resent it, or yourself, or your life.

Here's the part people skip, though: you have to actually *start*. You can spend weeks researching the perfect side hustle, comparing platforms, reading success stories, watching YouTube videos about passive income, and never actually do anything.

I see this all the time. Someone gets excited about freelance writing—great idea, totally viable—so they spend two weeks building the perfect Upwork profile. Agonizing over their bio. Choosing the right profile picture. Reading articles about how to write winning proposals. And then they never submit a single proposal because they're waiting to feel "ready."

You will never feel ready. You just have to be willing to be bad at it for a little while.

When Maria started freelance writing—this is a real person, someone I know—her first pitch on Upwork was terrible. She undercharged, overcommitted, and delivered a blog post that needed two rounds of revisions because she didn't really understand what the client wanted and was too nervous to ask clarifying questions. She made $25 and spent four hours on it. That's $6.25 an hour, well below minimum wage.

But she learned more from that one project than she did from three online courses. She learned what clients actually wanted (usually something simpler and more straightforward than she thought). She learned how long things really took (always longer than she estimated). She learned what she should charge next time ($40, then $75, then $100).

Her second project went smoother. Her fifth project, she charged $75 and finished in two hours. By her tenth, she was charging $150 and had a client who wanted four articles a month. That's $600 monthly, just from one repeat client—enough to cover her previous shortfalls and start building an actual emergency fund.

But none of that happens if she doesn't send that first terrible pitch.

So if you're sitting here thinking "I could probably do X, but I'm not good enough yet"—stop. You're good enough to start. You're not good enough to be *great* yet, but that's fine. Great comes later. Start comes now.

Pick one thing from your Skill column. Find one platform where people pay for that thing—Upwork, Fiverr, Thumbtack, TaskRabbit,

Facebook Marketplace, Nextdoor, Craigslist, wherever. Create a basic profile. It doesn't have to be perfect. It has to be done.

Then send one pitch. Post one listing. Reach out to one potential client.

One. Not ten. Not a perfect portfolio. One real attempt at earning money from this skill.

See what happens. Learn from it. Adjust. Try again.

Now I'm going to tell you something that might sound contradictory: sometimes the best income boost has nothing to do with working more.

Sometimes it's about working *differently*.

I talked earlier about asking for a raise at your current job. But there's a step before that most people miss: making yourself more valuable *first*. Not in some vague "be a better employee" way, but strategically.

Look at what skills are valued in your industry. Not what you wish were valued—what actually gets people promoted or paid more. Then acquire one of those skills. Just one.

If you work in an office and everyone's moving toward data-driven decision-making but you've never touched Excel beyond basic formulas—learn Excel. There are free courses. YouTube tutorials. Library resources. It'll take you maybe 20 hours to get competent enough to be useful. That's one month of dedicating 30-40 minutes a day. Less time than most people spend on Instagram.

Then start using it. Volunteer for a project that needs data analysis. Create a report that makes your boss's life easier. Solve a problem that's been annoying everyone but nobody had time to fix.

Make yourself the person they call when they need that thing done.

Six months later when you ask for a raise, you're not just saying "I've been here a while and I work hard." You're saying "I identified a gap, filled it, and here's the measurable value I've added." That's a completely different conversation. That's a conversation that's hard to say no to.

This works even if you're not in a traditional office job. If you're in retail and you notice the store's social media is a mess—or nonexistent—offer to help. Learn basic social media management (again: free resources everywhere) and pitch a simple plan. "I noticed we're not posting consistently on Instagram, and our competitors are getting a lot of engagement there. I could spend 30 minutes a day posting and responding to comments. Here's a sample content calendar."

You're not committing to becoming the full-time social media manager. You're solving a problem your manager probably knows exists but doesn't have time to fix.

If you're in food service and you see inefficiencies in how inventory is tracked—figure out a better system. If you're in healthcare and scheduling is a nightmare—find a solution, even a partial one.

You're not doing extra work for free forever. You're building leverage.

Because here's what most people don't realize: employers will almost always pay more to keep someone who solves problems than someone who just does their assigned tasks. The person who makes their manager's job easier, who sees what needs doing and does it, who brings solutions instead of just flagging issues—that person is expensive to replace. That person gets raises and promotions, not because they're better people, but because they're more valuable to the business.

Be that person. Document it. Then ask for compensation that reflects it.

Let's talk about online learning for a second, because I don't want you thinking you need to spend thousands of dollars on courses or go back to school for another degree.

You don't.

Coursera, edX, Khan Academy—all offer free courses from actual universities. MIT, Stanford, Yale—their courses are online, for free. YouTube has tutorials on literally everything. Your local library probably has a partnership with LinkedIn Learning or Skillshare or Creativebug. You can learn graphic design, coding, bookkeeping, digital marketing, copywriting, project management, whatever you want—for free or close to it.

The catch is you have to be self-directed. No one's going to hold you accountable. No one's going to give you a deadline or grade your work or send you reminder emails. You have to decide what you're learning, block out the time, and follow through even when you don't feel like it.

So pick one skill. One. Not five. Not "I'm going to learn coding AND graphic design AND copywriting AND photography." One thing that's either directly useful in your current job or marketable as a side income stream.

Then commit to 30 minutes a day. That's it. Not two hours when you're motivated on Sunday afternoon and then nothing for a week. Thirty minutes every single day, even if you're tired, even if you'd rather scroll your phone, even if you can only do it at 10 PM after the kids are asleep.

Thirty minutes a day is 3.5 hours a week. Fifteen hours a month. In two months you'll have put in 30 focused hours of learning. That's enough to go from "I've never done this" to "I'm competent enough to get paid for this" in most practical skills. Not an expert. Still learning. But competent enough to deliver value and get paid.

It won't make you the best in the field. You'll still be learning on the job, still Googling things, still occasionally feeling like you have no idea what you're doing.

But it'll get you in the door. It'll get you that first client, that first project, that first $50 or $100 you earned from a skill you didn't have two months ago.

And that's all you need—to get in the door and start earning.

Here's the thing nobody tells you about income boosting, the part that's frustrating but important: it's not a one-time fix.

You don't just ask for a raise once, or start a side hustle once, and then you're done forever and your financial problems are solved and you never have to think about money again.

Your financial situation changes. Your expenses go up. Rent increases. Your car needs replacing. Your kid needs braces. Medical bills happen. The gap reappears, or a new gap opens up, or you get to a stable place and then life happens and you're back to struggling.

So this isn't a chapter you read, implement, and forget. It's a strategy you return to every 6-12 months. You reassess. You ask yourself: Am I still being paid what I'm worth, or has my role expanded while my salary stayed flat? Are there new skills I should be learning that would make me more valuable? Is my side income still sustainable or has it become a burden I resent? Should I be actively looking for a better-paying job, or is the current one still the right fit?

The goal isn't to constantly hustle forever, to work 80-hour weeks for the rest of your life. The goal is to close the gap between what you earn and what you need, then close it again when it reappears, until eventually—and this can take years, I'm not going to lie to you—you're not in triage mode anymore.

Until you have margin. Until one unexpected expense doesn't derail your entire month. Until you can go to dinner with friends and order what you actually want instead of the cheapest thing on the menu. Until someone asks if you want to chip in $20 for a group gift and you just say yes without mentally rearranging your budget.

That's when budgeting advice from normal personal finance books finally becomes useful. That's when you can think about retirement accounts and investment strategies and optimizing your credit card rewards and all the stuff that sounds absurd—borderline insulting—when you're $280 short and sitting at your kitchen table at midnight wondering which bill you can push to next month.

But you don't start there. You start here—with the immediate problem of not enough money coming in.

You fix that first. Everything else gets easier after.

So here's what I want you to think about, not tonight necessarily, maybe tomorrow or the next day when you have a quiet moment:

What would your life look like with an extra $300 a month?

Not $3,000. Not "what if I won the lottery." Just $300.

Would that close your gap? Would that let you stop pushing bills to next month? Would that mean you could buy your kid the shoes they need without having to choose between that and groceries? Would it mean you could finally start putting something, even just $50, into savings so the next emergency doesn't completely wreck you?

$300 a month is $75 a week. It's one $50 freelance article plus a $25 task. It's two small cooking classes. It's the difference between a $42,000 salary and a $45,600 salary—a raise that's absolutely achievable if you document your value and ask for it.

It's not out of reach. It's not reserved for people with college degrees or special connections or some talent you don't have. It's available to you, right now, if you're willing to try.

Not willing to be perfect at it. Willing to try. Willing to send the imperfect pitch, have the uncomfortable conversation, spend 30 minutes a day learning something new even though you're tired.

Because here's what I've seen, over and over: the people who change their financial situation aren't the smartest people or the most talented people or the people with the most advantages.

They're the people who decided the gap wasn't acceptable anymore and took one small action toward closing it.

And then another. And another.

Until the kitchen table at midnight stopped being the place where they realized the math didn't work, and started being the place where they built something different.

More income helps—it's not a moral failing to need it. But income alone won't save a system that leaks, and without a system to hold it all together, every strategy you've learned stays theoretical.

You've cut everything you can cut. You've negotiated what you can negotiate. You've built forecasting into your system. And now you're earning $300 more per month than three months ago. The gap is closing. The question is: how do you hold onto this when life throws you the next curveball?

Chapter 9: Putting It All Together: The 'Monthly Money Map'

It's 11 PM on a Tuesday and you're sitting at your kitchen table with four different notebooks, two apps fighting for space on your phone screen, and a stack of bills that arrived over the past three weeks. You've learned to prioritize, negotiate, find hidden money, build a buffer, and forecast what's coming. You know where every dollar goes. The question now is: how do all these pieces actually work together?

Remember the $12.99 streaming charge from Chapter 5—the one you'd been paying for eleven months without watching? It's still canceled. And now you see every subscription before it renews, every recurring charge before it hits, because your system flags them before they bleed you dry.

But you don't.

Here's what you *do* have: the income tracking from Chapter 2 is solid—you know exactly what hits your account and when. The Bill Priority Matrix from Chapter 3 lives on a sticky note stuck to your fridge, right next to the takeout menu you haven't used in two months because you're trying to be smart about money. Last week you negotiated with the electric company using one of those scripts from Chapter 4, and that felt weirdly good—like maybe you're getting the hang of this—but now you can't remember if you wrote down the new payment date or just thought really hard about writing it down. The Gap Closer list exists somewhere in your phone's notes app. You think. Your buffer fund is either at $340 or maybe $180 because you might have pulled from it when your car needed tires, but you're not actually sure if you marked that anywhere.

This is the part nobody warned me about when I started trying to fix my money situation. Not that the tactics don't work—they do. I know they work because I've watched them work, in my life and in other people's. The problem is you're running eight different systems simultaneously inside your head, and your head wasn't built to be a financial command center operating 24/7.

Let me tell you what that actually costs. Real dollars, not metaphors.

You miss the $45 phone bill. Not because you're irresponsible, but because you were tracking the big stuff—rent, car payment, insurance—and the medium stuff slipped through. Phone bill triggers a $20 late fee. You wouldn't have paid that $20 if you'd just remembered, except you can't "just remember" when you're simultaneously tracking income across three different gig apps, mentally calculating whether you can afford groceries this week or need to stretch what's in the pantry another four days, trying to remember if that creditor said the 15th or the 18th for the modified payment, wondering if your roommate Venmo'd you their half of utilities yet, and—

You get the idea. Your brain is full.

The mental load itself costs money. I'm not being poetic here. When you're using brain space to remember whether you moved money from checking to savings or just meant to move it, you're not fully present at your actual job. You miss details. You're slower to respond. And if you're doing work where tips matter, or where managers notice who's sharp and who's perpetually distracted? That's money you're not making because you're trying to hold your entire financial life in working memory like some kind of human spreadsheet.

Or you make mistakes that cost you directly. This happened to me last year. I thought I had $180 in checking because I forgot to mark down a $40 Venmo to my sister for her birthday. Bought groceries. Card declined at the register. I'm standing there, face hot, apologizing to the cashier while the guy behind me sighs loud enough that everyone in line can hear it. Left half my groceries on the counter and walked out. The shame was free, at least. The overdraft fee—because that gas station charge from two days ago cleared right after the grocery store's transaction tried to process—was $35.

Thirty-five dollars. Gone. Because I was holding too much in my head and something fell out.

This is what it feels like to have tactics without a system. Not failing because the tools are bad. Failing because you're juggling them separately, and every few days you drop one, and every single drop costs you something.

I know what you're thinking, because I thought it too: "Great. Another system. Another thing I'm going to start with good intentions and abandon in three weeks when life gets messy."

Fair. If I'm asking you to add another layer of maintenance to your already-full plate, we have a problem. But here's the thing—this isn't adding work. It's consolidating work you're already doing. Everything you're tracking in your head, on random apps, on sticky notes, in text files on your phone that you titled "BUDGET FINAL VERSION 3" six months ago and haven't opened since? All of that is going to live in one place. One document. One weekly check-in instead of this constant background hum of mental accounting that never actually shuts off.

I call it the Monthly Money Map, and it's less like a traditional budget—which always felt to me like being told to build a house when what I needed was a flashlight to find my way through the dark—and more like a GPS. Not the kind that makes you plan every single turn for the entire month. The kind that shows you where you are right now, where you need to end up, and what route makes sense given current conditions. Traffic changes. Roads close. You adjust. Same principle here.

The core is simple. One document—digital, paper, whatever format doesn't make you want to ignore it—that shows your entire monthly income and expense cycle. Not just what you spend, but *when* money comes in, *when* it goes out, and what you do when those two timelines don't line up nicely. Because they never do.

Start at the top with predictable income. That's anything you can reasonably count on: your main job, regular side gigs that actually show up every month, child support if it genuinely arrives reliably. Notice I didn't say "expected income" or "projected income." I said *predictable*. If it's not at least 90% certain, it doesn't go here.

Why the hard line? Because the single biggest mistake people make with variable income is budgeting for the best-case scenario. I did this for two years straight. Look at the last three months—brought in $2,100, then $2,800, then $2,400—and you think, "Okay, I'll budget for $2,500. That's reasonable, right? It's close to the average." Then you have a $1,900 month and your whole plan collapses like a house of cards in a stiff breeze.

Budget for the floor instead. What's the lowest amount you've brought in over the last six months? That's your predictable income number. I know it feels almost depressing to write down $1,900 when you've been averaging $2,400. Do it anyway. Better to be pleasantly surprised than constantly scrambling. And here's something nobody tells you: writing down the lower number doesn't make it more likely to happen. It just means you're prepared when it does. That's not pessimism. That's realism when the math is already tight.

Below predictable income, create a section called Variable Income. This is everything else: freelance projects that haven't actually landed yet, gig work, overtime that depends on whether your boss approves it, that bonus someone mentioned in passing but hasn't confirmed in writing. Do not—and I'm completely serious about this—do not fold this money into your spending plan yet. It doesn't exist until it's in your account. Once it clears? We'll deal with it. But this section isn't about planning. It's about tracking what actually shows up.

Think of Variable Income as the section where hope meets reality. Hope says you'll bring in an extra $600 this month from that side gig. Reality says maybe you will, maybe you won't, maybe the client will pay you in six weeks instead of two. Track it when it lands. Not before.

Now we get to expenses, and this is where all that prioritization work from earlier chapters pays off. Three categories. They're not equal, and they're not treated equally, and pretending they are is how people end up in overdraft while their Spotify subscription renews.

Must-Haves: rent or mortgage, utilities, minimum transportation to keep your job, basic groceries. Not the groceries you want. The ones that keep you fed. The number here should make you slightly uncomfortable. If you're looking at it thinking, "Well that's not much of a life," you're probably doing it right. This isn't your life. This is the floor—what you need when income hits its lowest point. Everything else is built on top of this, but this is the foundation that doesn't crack.

Important But Flexible: internet (and yes, it's important, but you could downgrade the speed if you absolutely had to), insurance, minimum debt payments beyond what's already in Must-Haves, phone bill, childcare. These matter. Pay them whenever possible. But in a true crisis month—when income falls short and you're choosing between bad options—some of these can be negotiated, delayed, or temporarily reduced. That doesn't make them frivolous. It makes them flexible. There's a difference.

Wants: streaming services, eating out, hobbies, the actually-good coffee beans instead of the Folgers, anything that falls into "nice to have." I'm not telling you to eliminate these forever. I'm not one of those financial people who thinks you should live like a monk for five years so you can retire at 40. I'm telling you to know exactly what they cost and be ready to cut them when you need to.

Here's where people usually push back: "But I need my phone for work, so that should be Must-Have, not Important But Flexible."

Maybe. But do you need the $80 unlimited data plan, or would the $35 limited plan work for nine months out of the year? Categorizing something as Flexible doesn't mean it's frivolous or that you don't really need it. It means there's a cheaper version available if you hit a genuinely bad month. That distinction matters when you're $340 short and trying to figure out what stays and what goes.

Under your expense categories, you need a permanent line item called Buffer Zone. We talked about building this back in Chapter 6, but now it gets a fixed spot on your map. This is money you've set aside—ideally one to two weeks of essential expenses—that sits in your checking account as a cushion. Not in savings where you have to transfer it. In checking, right there, ready. When income dips or an unexpected expense hits, the buffer absorbs it. No scrambling to figure out which bill doesn't get paid this month. No calling your mom at 9 PM asking to borrow $200. Pull from the buffer, and then—this is the critical part most people miss—you refill it as soon as Variable Income comes in.

The buffer is what keeps you from living in constant crisis mode. It's the difference between a $280 car repair being a problem you solve and a $280 car repair being a catastrophe that derails your entire month.

Which brings us to what you actually do with Variable Income when it shows up.

First priority, always: replenish the buffer to its target level. If your buffer should be $600 and it's currently sitting at $400, the first $200 of any extra income goes there. Non-negotiable. The buffer is what keeps this whole system from falling apart the first time something unexpected happens. And something unexpected always happens. Your kid needs new shoes. The prescription costs more than you thought. Your hours get cut for two weeks because business is slow. The buffer is what stands between you and a payday loan.

Second priority: debt above minimums, using whichever method you chose—snowball or avalanche. Even $25 extra toward your smallest debt creates momentum. It's not much, but it's movement, and movement matters when you've been stuck.

Third priority: emergency fund. This is different from the buffer. The buffer lives in checking and gets used regularly—that's its job. The emergency fund lives in savings and only gets touched for true emergencies: medical bills, car breakdown, job loss, things that would otherwise send you straight to a credit card or a payday loan. Building toward three to six months of essential expenses eventually, but start with $500. Then $1,000. Work your way up in chunks you can see and reach.

Let me show you what this looks like in practice, because Sarah—a freelance graphic designer I know, someone who's given me permission to share her situation because she thinks it might help people—actually uses this system, and her income fluctuates so wildly that watching it used to stress me out just hearing about it.

Sarah's predictable income is $800 a month. That's it. One client pays her a small monthly retainer for social media graphics, and that's the only thing she can genuinely count on. Everything else—and she averages another $1,200 to $2,000 a month in project work depending on how busy things are—goes in Variable Income. It shows up when it shows up, which is sometimes prompt and sometimes six weeks after she sends an invoice because small businesses run on chaos and hope.

Her Must-Haves total $1,400: rent is $800 (she lives with two roommates in a city where that's actually a deal), utilities average $150, she needs a car to meet clients so transportation is $150 for insurance and gas, and she's got groceries at $300.

Notice something? Her predictable income doesn't even cover Must-Haves. She's $600 short every single month before we even get to her phone bill or student loans.

This is why the traditional budgeting advice—"just track your expenses and trim the fat"—falls apart for people in Sarah's situation. There is no fat. She already cut to bone. She's not eating out. She's not buying clothes. Her "fun money" is the $15 she spends at Target once a month when she needs to feel like a human being instead of a debt-repayment machine. The problem isn't budgeting. It's income volatility, and you can't budget your way out of that without a completely different system.

So here's what Sarah's Map looks like in a typical month. Predictable income: $800. Must-Haves: $1,400. That $600 gap gets filled by Variable Income—but she doesn't know when it's coming. A client might pay her on the 5th. Or the 19th. Or, if they're running their own cash flow crisis, not until the 3rd of the next month, which leaves her short for weeks.

Her Important But Flexible category runs another $400: internet ($75, and she needs decent speed for sending design files), health insurance ($200, the cheapest plan she could find on the marketplace), and student loan minimum payment ($125). Wants are kept tight at around $300: she eats out maybe twice a month, has Netflix and Spotify, buys art supplies occasionally because that's what keeps her sane and remotely connected to why she became a designer in the first place.

Total monthly expenses: $2,100. Average monthly income: $2,000 to $2,800. On paper, she should be fine. She's bringing in more than she's spending most months.

In reality, six months ago, she was drowning.

What changed? She stopped budgeting based on monthly totals and started budgeting based on cash flow timing. Because when you're broke, timing is everything. It's not about how much you make. It's about when it hits your account relative to when bills are due. That gap—between money coming in and money needing to go out—is where people drown, and most budgeting advice pretends it doesn't exist.

Her rent is due on the 1st. Her predictable $800 hits her account on the 1st. She immediately pays rent. Now she's at zero, with $600 of Must-Haves still unpaid, plus everything else looming.

She usually has a project payment of $500 to $700 that hits around the 10th. Let's say it's $600. That covers the rest of Must-Haves. Now we're at the 10th, she's covered the essentials, and she's back to zero.

Another $400 typically comes in around the 20th. That covers Important But Flexible. We're at the 20th now, and she's still at zero in her checking account.

See the problem? Even in a decent month where she brings in $2,400 total, she's living at zero balance until the very end of the month. Any unexpected expense—and there's always an unexpected expense—sends her into overdraft or onto a credit card. A parking ticket. Cat needs flea medication. Friend's birthday and she can't show up empty-handed without feeling like garbage. Any of it, and she's underwater.

The Buffer Zone fixed this. Sarah built up $700 over three months—one week's worth of essential expenses—and she keeps it in checking. Just sits there. Doesn't get touched unless she absolutely needs it. Now when rent comes due on the 1st, she pays it, but she's not at zero. She's at $700.

The psychological difference is enormous. She's not in crisis mode every single day of every single month. She can breathe.

And when Variable Income hits? The very first thing she does is check: is the buffer still at $700? If she had to pull $200 from it for a car repair, the first $200 of the next payment goes right back into the buffer. Only after that does she allocate to debt, savings, or Wants.

This is what I mean when I talk about anticipatory budgeting (and yes, I know that sounds like consultant-speak, but I don't have a better term for it). Sarah's not reacting to her income anymore. She's not in constant firefighting mode. She's planned for the volatility before it happens, so when it happens—and it always happens—she's got a system to handle it instead of just stress and panic and a credit card she swore she wouldn't use again.

Now let me walk you through the weekly maintenance routine, because this is where consistency matters more than perfection. Way more. And I need to be honest with you about something: this part is boring. There's no hack here. No shortcut. It's just showing up every week and doing the thing, even when you don't feel like it, even when it's the last thing you want to do after working all week.

Every Sunday—or Saturday, or Monday night, or whatever day works for your actual life, but make it the same day every single week—you review. Pull up your Money Map. Look at what came in over the past seven days and mark it in the Variable Income section. Look at what went out and make sure it matches what you planned. If you overspent in one category, don't spiral. Just note it. Awareness is the first step toward change. Beating yourself up is optional and, in my experience, completely unhelpful. I've never met anyone who budgeted better because they hated themselves more. Doesn't work that way.

Then look ahead to the next seven days. What bills are due? What income do you expect? Are there any gaps where money needs to go out before money comes in?

If you see a potential problem—say, your car insurance is due on Thursday but your paycheck doesn't hit until Friday—you solve it now, while you have time and options. Maybe you move $140 from the buffer and plan to replace it Friday afternoon. Maybe you call the insurance company and ask to shift your due date by three days, which most of them will do if you just ask. The point is, you're not discovering the problem when your card declines at the grocery store. Saw it coming a week out. Had time to fix it.

I've been using a version of this system for three years now, and here's what I've learned: the format matters way less than the habit. Some people swear by spreadsheets with color-coded cells and automatic calculations that make them feel like they're working at NASA. Others use budgeting apps that link to their bank accounts and send you cheerful notifications about spending. I've seen people do this effectively with a spiral notebook and a pen, just writing it out by hand every week because that's what makes it feel real to them. The tool is not the point. The weekly review is the point.

Pick whatever format you'll actually use. Not the one that sounds impressive. Not the one your friend swears by. The one you'll open every single week even when you're tired and don't want to.

And here's the thing nobody tells you about financial systems, the thing that took me way too long to figure out: they fail. Not because they're bad systems. Not because you're doing it wrong. But because life is chaotic and unpredictable and sometimes genuinely unfair, and no system survives contact with reality completely intact.

You'll have a week where you forget to review. You'll have a month where an emergency blows through your buffer like a wrecking ball and you have to rebuild from absolute zero. You'll make a purchase you regret—I bought a $60 video game two months ago when I knew I shouldn't have, and I still feel dumb about it every time I see it sitting there unplayed—and have to adjust. This is all completely normal. Expected, even. The system isn't about perfection. It's about having a place to return to when things go sideways.

Sarah had a month where three different clients paid late—not because they were trying to screw her over, just because businesses are chaotic and AP departments move slowly and sometimes invoices get lost in someone's email and you have to send it again with a polite "just checking in!" message that makes you feel like you're begging for money you already earned. Same month, her cat needed an emergency vet visit ($340), and her car needed new tires ($280). Her carefully built $700 buffer got obliterated. Wiped out completely. She was back in crisis mode, pulling out a credit card for the vet bill because what else was she supposed to do, let the cat suffer?

And you know what? She didn't abandon the system. Didn't throw up her hands and say, "See? This doesn't work for people like me." She just started rebuilding. Slowly. $50 one week. $80 the next. $30 the week after that when a client paid early and she could spare it. Back into the buffer, bit by bit. Took her two full months to get back to $700, but she got there. Because the system isn't fragile. It bends. It absorbs hits. It rebuilds.

That's the thing traditional financial advice gets completely wrong. They act like once you set up a budget, you're done. Fixed your finances. Can move on to the next life improvement project—maybe start meal prepping or learning a language or whatever productive people do. But managing money when you're broke—when the math is tight and there's no margin for error—isn't a one-time fix. It's an ongoing practice. The Money Map isn't a destination you reach. It's infrastructure. It's the road you walk every single week, and some weeks the road is smooth and some weeks there's construction everywhere and detours and potholes, but you keep walking because it's still better than being lost in the dark.

Now let me give you the actual worksheet template, because talking about this in theory is one thing, but you need to build yours today. Not next week. Not when things calm down—things are never going to calm down, that's not how life works. Today, before you close this chapter and move on to something else and tell yourself you'll come back to it later and then three months pass and you're still carrying your entire financial life in your head.

Monthly Money Map

I. Predictable Income: * Source 1 (job, retainer, etc.): $_________ * Source 2: $_________ * Source 3: $_________ * **Total Predictable: $_________**

II. Variable Income (Track Weekly): * Week 1 (1st-7th): $_________ * Week 2 (8th-14th): $_________ * Week 3 (15th-21st): $_________ * Week 4 (22nd-end): $_________ * **Total Variable This Month: $_________**

III. Expenses:

A. Must-Haves (The Floor): * Rent/Mortgage: $_________ * Utilities (electric, water, gas): $_________ * Transportation (car payment, insurance, gas, or transit pass): $_________ * Basic Groceries: $_________ * Other non-negotiables: $_________ * **Subtotal Must-Haves: $_________**

B. Important But Flexible: * Internet: $_________ * Phone: $_________ * Insurance (health, renters, etc.): $_________ * Minimum debt payments: $_________ * Childcare: $_________ * Other: $_________ * **Subtotal Important But Flexible: $_________**

C. Wants: * Streaming services: $_________ * Eating out: $_________ * Hobbies/entertainment: $_________ * Other discretionary: $__________ * **Subtotal Wants: $__________**

IV. Buffer Zone: * Current buffer balance: $__________ * Target buffer amount (1-2 weeks of Must-Haves): $__________ * Gap to close: $__________

V. When Variable Income Arrives: 1. Refill buffer to target: $__________ 2. Extra debt payment: $__________ 3. Emergency fund contribution: $__________ 4. Everything else

Fill this out. Right now would be good, but if you genuinely can't—if you're reading this on a lunch break or before bed and don't have your numbers in front of you—then put a reminder in your phone for the next time you're home with 30 minutes free. Treat it like a doctor's appointment. Non-negotiable. Because every week you operate without this is another week where you're relying on memory and hope and luck, and eventually one of those fails.

Here's what happened when I finally sat down and built my first Money Map three years ago: I found $340 I didn't know I was spending. Not in one big place. In eight small places. Subscriptions I forgot about. Apps that charged $4.99 a month and I never noticed. A gym membership I hadn't used in four months but kept paying because canceling felt like admitting defeat. None of it was dramatic. All of it added up. And seeing it written down—seeing the actual total at the bottom of the page—made it real in a way that vaguely knowing I was "probably spending too much on stuff" never did.

The Money Map won't fix your income problem. If you're bringing in $1,800 a month and your Must-Haves are $2,200, a better tracking system won't close that $400 gap. You still need the income-boosting strategies from Chapter 8. You still need to negotiate with creditors when necessary. You still need to make hard choices about what gets paid and what doesn't. But what the Map does—what it's designed to do—is stop you from losing money you already have to disorganization, forgotten bills, overdraft fees, and the constant mental drain of trying to hold everything in your head at once.

It gives you clarity. And when money is tight, clarity is worth something. Worth more than you'd think, actually. Because you can't solve a problem you can't see clearly, and most people living paycheck to paycheck are operating in a fog of partial information and best guesses and hoping it all works out somehow. The Map clears the fog. Shows you exactly where you are, exactly what's coming, exactly what needs to happen between now and the end of the month.

And then—this is the part that surprised me—it shows you what's actually possible. Once Sarah had her Map built and running for three months, she could see patterns she'd never noticed before. She could see that March and April were always her slowest months for freelance work, so she started saving extra in January and February to cover the gap. She could see that she was spending $180 a month on groceries in weeks when she meal-prepped and $340 in weeks when she didn't, which made the hour she spent on Sunday afternoons chopping vegetables feel less like a chore and more like a $160-a-month raise. She could see that one specific client always paid 30 days late, every single time, which meant she could plan for that instead of being surprised by it every month and scrambling to cover bills.

The Map didn't change her income. Didn't change her expenses, really. Changed what she could see, and what you can see, you can work with.

One last thing, and then I'll let you go build yours: the first month is going to feel clunky. Your numbers won't be perfect. You'll forget to mark something down. You'll realize halfway through the month that you categorized something wrong and now your totals don't make sense. That's fine. Expected, even. Month two will be smoother. Month three, smoother still. By month four, you'll be doing this in 15 minutes on Sunday morning with your coffee, barely thinking about it, because it's just what you do now.

Sarah told me something a few months after she started using this system. Said she'd gone to the grocery store and her card declined—some payment timing issue, nothing dramatic—and instead of that hot rush of shame and panic she used to feel, she just thought, "Oh, I pulled from the buffer this week for that car thing. I'll transfer money over when I get home." Paid cash. Walked out. Didn't think about it again. That shift—from shame and panic to just solving the problem—is what this system is built for. Not perfection. Not never having problems. Just having a framework that turns problems into solvable logistics instead of personal failures that keep you up at 2 AM wondering how you're going to make it through the month.

Build your Map. Use it every week. Let it fail sometimes, then rebuild it. Watch what changes when you can finally see clearly what's actually happening with your money instead of just feeling anxious about it in the background all the time.

And after you've used this for a month or two, after the system starts to feel like second nature instead of another obligation you're trying to keep up with—that's when something interesting happens. The Map stops being just a tracking tool and becomes a planning tool. You start to see not just where you are, but where you could be three months from now if you make different choices. That extra $50 from Variable Income stops feeling like "finally, breathing room" and starts feeling like a decision point: buffer, debt, or emergency fund? Each choice visible. Each outcome predictable. The fog cleared for good.

Because here's what most budgeting systems miss: they're designed for month one. They're built to help you survive your first encounter with your spending, to categorize things correctly, to feel like you're finally getting a handle on it. But they don't scale up. They don't tell you what happens when the system works, when you've been using it long enough that the basic mechanics fade into the background and you start using it for something bigger.

The Monthly Money Map scales. Once you've mapped three months in a row, you start to see patterns you couldn't see before. Not just "I spend too much on groceries"—you knew that already. But patterns like: you always underestimate Irregular Expenses in months that have birthdays. Or your Variable Income drops in summer but your Fixed Costs don't, so July is always tighter than you thought it would be. Or that $200 you've been putting toward debt every month has actually cleared three small accounts in six months, and now you could consolidate what's left into one payment and free up mental space.

These aren't insights you can get from one month. They're the kind of thing that only emerges when you have continuity, when each month's Map builds on the last one and you can flip back and compare. And that's when the real shift happens—when you stop asking "Can I afford this?" and start asking "What does this do to next month's Map?"

Let's say you get an unexpected $300. Maybe it's a tax refund, maybe it's freelance work you forgot was coming, maybe someone finally paid you back. Before the Map, that $300 would've felt like permission. Permission to go out to dinner without checking the bank account first. Permission to buy the thing you've been talking yourself out of for two months. Permission to relax about money for five minutes.

And there's nothing wrong with any of that, by the way. But with the Map, you have a different option. You can pull up next month's draft—because yes, you're already sketching next month while you're living this one—and you can see exactly what that $300 does. Does it cover the Gap you were worried about? Does it let you move something out of the Irregular Expenses anxiety column and into the "handled" column? Does it mean you can actually take that weekend trip in two months instead of just hoping it works out?

The difference is visibility. The $300 isn't just relief anymore. It's a tool. And you're the one deciding what it builds.

Or let's say the opposite happens. Let's say your car needs $400 worth of work and you don't have $400 just sitting around waiting for this exact emergency. Most people hit that moment and spiral. They put it on a credit card, or they skip paying something else this month and hope they can catch up next month, or they borrow from a friend and add "figure out how to pay them back" to the growing list of financial stress they're already carrying.

With the Map, you still don't have $400. The Map didn't magic money into existence. But you do have options you can actually see. You can look at your Irregular Expenses for the next two months and see what's flexible. You can look at your Variable Income projection and know whether you're expecting anything that could cover part of it. You can look at your Buffer and make an informed decision about whether pulling from it now means you'll be okay next month or whether it leaves you too exposed. You can even look at your debt payments and decide—just this once, just for this specific reason—to pay minimums for one month so the $400 doesn't turn into $600 on a credit card.

None of those options are perfect. But they're all better than panic. And they're all choices you can make because you can see the consequences before they happen.

That's what the Map gives you. Not control over what happens—you're never going to control that—but control over how you respond. And over time, that changes everything.

Because once you're not spending half your energy just reacting to whatever fire is burning loudest, you have space to think about what you actually want your money to do. Not in some vague "someday I'll be financially stable" way, but in a specific, this-year-this-is-the-goal way.

Maybe that's building your Emergency Fund to three months of expenses instead of one. Maybe it's paying off the credit card that's been sitting at $2,000 for two years. Maybe it's saving for a trip, or a certification program, or a down payment, or just getting to the end of a month without that pit-in-your-stomach feeling when you check your account balance.

The Map doesn't care what the goal is. It just shows you whether you're moving toward it or away from it, month by month. And if you're moving away from it, it shows you why. Not in a judgmental "you're bad with money" way, but in a factual "your Fixed Costs went up but your Base Income didn't, so something has to give" way.

And that clarity—that boring, undramatic, just-the-facts clarity—is weirdly powerful. Because once you know why something isn't working, you can fix it. Or you can decide not to fix it, because the tradeoff is worth it, but at least you decided. You weren't just swept along.

So here's what happens after a few months of using the Monthly Money Map: you stop feeling like money is something that happens to you. It's still hard sometimes. There are still months where everything costs more than you planned and you have to make uncomfortable decisions. But those months don't break you anymore, because you saw them coming, or because you have a plan for recovering from them, or because you know exactly what you're sacrificing and why.

And the months that go well—the ones where your Variable Income is higher than expected, or you didn't need as much for Irregular Expenses, or you just made it through without any disasters—those months don't disappear into nothing anymore. You don't get to the end and think "wait, where did it all go?" You know where it went. And you decided where the extra went. And that decision is still working for you next month, and the month after that.

That's the shift. That's what it feels like when the system is working. Not like you suddenly have more money. Not like your problems are solved. But like you're finally driving instead of being driven. And once you feel that, once you've had even one month where you knew what was happening and made real choices and saw them work—you don't go back. You can't. Because now you know what's possible.

Also in the Series

Every book in Money Reset stands on its own — read them in any order. If this one was useful, the library continues:

Tax Strategies to Keep What You Earn

Salary Negotiation Before You Sign

Budgeting for People Who Hate Budgeting

Budgeting From Zero

Budgeting on an Irregular Income

Couples Budgeting

Budgeting After Debt

Budgeting Without a Spreadsheet

Budgeting for Impulse Spending

Budgeting for a Bigger Life